Addicted to Love

Advance Praise

for yourself and holds space for you to be you. She has you examine the 'why' of what you do so that you can then choose the path you most desire. She practices what she preaches and stands as a witness that recovery is definitely possible and doable. I sure wish I had a book like this that focused on the bigger picture and a wholehearted approach while going through the rough and choppy recovery process. These tools and how they are presented are truly life changing. She calls me on my crap, and I love it!"

-Emily C.

"In this book, Lacy is like the big sister you never had: been there, done that, and here to tell it like it is and help you walk a better path. Her honesty and humor are always balanced with empathy and encouragement to sustain you on your journey to recovery. I'm grateful for the validation and guidance she has offered regarding this lesser-recognized addiction. I no longer feel alone."

-F.N.

"As a woman in recovery, I have often been frustrated by the scarcity of resources written specifically for women. I used to feel like I must be the only woman who struggled with sexual addictions. As I have progressed in my recovery, I have learned that there are many women who have faced struggles similar to mine who are now living lives of authenticity and peace. With this book, Lacy has given women another resource to help us find the healing we are looking for. It's not easy. Lacy includes an entire chapter on the courage it takes to live in alignment with the things we desire most in our lives. But it is possible, and incorporating into our lives the principles found in this book can help us achieve the healing and freedom we are looking for."

-Jenny T.

From Former Clients and Other Women:

"Lacy pushes you to truly understand your values and worth. Whether or not you know Lacy on a personal basis, she makes you feel like she is one of your closest friends, offering her support and guidance through every step of your recovery. She doesn't beat around the bush – she is honest about how to accept your vulnerability and imperfections, and how to break free from the fantasies that have held you back for so long. I encourage anyone who is struggling to talk to, then listen to her. Thank you for sharing your experiences and wisdom, Lacy!"

-Nicole K

"After many years of sponsoring women struggling with an addiction that hardly anything is known about, Lacy compiled the best of her extensive knowledge and experience of what it takes to recover into one place. Her light, friendly conversational writing style feels like the reader is being instructed by a loving sister or beloved friend while also maintaining a very accountable look into thoughts motives and behaviors behind lust. The reader can count on this book to shed light on all the corners that have previously remained dark, taboo, or unpopular to public opinion."

-M.J.

"Lacy has a fantastic way of pointing out the places we tend to overlook as women struggling with this addiction. When I began my recovery, I needed the honesty that Lacy provides from her experiences. I am grateful for the encouraging hope that she provides."

-Leone N.

"I feel like even though this is geared for married, heterosexual women, this book is really for any young woman or woman desiring to be their whole self, and it can be applied to any number of 'distractions'. I'm grateful there wasn't the 'I'm an addict' sentiment in it either like so many other recovery resources I've read over the years. To me it feels empowering to call it and name it for exactly what it is, a distraction. That alone means I am powerful beyond measure and I'm no longer at the mercy, or in a place of victimhood regarding the often very charged word called 'addiction.'"

-Kathryn C.

"She is such a clarity wavelength. I wish I could just keep her in my pocket!"

-A.C.

"Lacy is able to provide light to a topic that tends to be so dark and lonely. Reading her book was like listening to a concerned friend, and the values she discusses can be applied to many aspects of life. *Addicted to Love* is one of those books that you can't help but come away from it a better woman. No matter what addiction you are battling, if any, Lacy's story will start you down a journey of recovery you didn't realize you needed."

-Shaylin D.

From the Professionals:

"Lacy has found a balance between candidly expressing herself while still exercising sensitivity for her reader. Her words are encouraging and uplifting. I particularly appreciated the workbook element of the book. She offers substantial action steps that are easy to understand and at least begin to use.

I recommend her book to those who are at any point in going through their own recovery. Any addict to a fantasy life that interferes with reality will benefit by reading and applying these principles. I will also be recommending this book to those who work or live with clients or family members with known relationship or sexual addictions. As they experience this book, they will understand more accurately and compassionately. Many will realize they have their own addictive or damaging thought and behavior patterns to work on."

-Dr. Carol Lynn Baker

"A reflective journey into the author's own experiences add a poignant measure of compassion to this empowering, uplifting book, while the values-based exercises provide meaningful, applicable activities to support the reader's recovery process. *Addicted to Love* is an insightful introspection that may benefit individuals experiencing other compulsive or obsessive behaviors and thoughts - as well as those who are within the support circle of loved ones seeking recovery."

-Jessica D. Egbert, PhD

"Lacy brings a feminine voice and perspective to a long-ignored problem that affects women and their relationships. Many women who are traumatized by past experiences crave what they think is love. *Addicted to Love* is a valuable roadmap to recovery and connecting with your authentic self in relationships. Lacy's voice of experience brings refreshing honesty, hope, and personal encouragement directly to your life. By understanding the "why" of what you do, you can stop waiting to have a prince rescue you, then begin to rescue yourself."

-Dr. A.J. Panos

"*Addicted to Love* is an interactive and thought-provoking book for any woman looking for further guidance in their life and marriage. Lacy is stocked with questions that truly explore the definition and world of living in 'fantasy'".

-Tennessa Harmon, M.S., ACMHC

"*Addicted to Love* shines with a powerful combination of a pioneer's passion – 'Lacy has been helping women heal from these issues since 2000' – and the hard-won wisdom of having *been there herself.* Along the way, she's learned a ton about that elusive quality so many women search for in relationships with men: happiness. Her recipe challenges even as it rings true, offering readers a road map out of fantasy and onto the painful, yet productive path to REAL love. *Addicted to Love* is an inspired how-to invitation to adventure; I highly recommend it!"

-Staci Sprout, LICSW, CSAT,
author of *Naked in Public: A Memoir of Recovery from Sex Addiction and Other Temporary Insanities*

Addicted
to
Love

Recovery, Empowerment and
Finding Your True Self

LACY ALAJNA BENTLEY

NEW YORK

LONDON • NASHVILLE • MELBOURNE • VANCOUVER

Addicted to *Love*

Recovery, Empowerment, and Finding Your True Self

Published in New York, New York, by Morgan James Publishing. Morgan James is a trademark of Morgan James, LLC. www.MorganJamesPublishing.com

ISBN 9781642792881 paperback
ISBN 9781642792898 eBook
Library of Congress Control Number: 2018911374

Cover Design & Interior Design by:
Christopher Kirk
www.GFSstudio.com

Morgan James is a proud partner of Habitat for Humanity Peninsula
and Greater Williamsburg. Partners in building since 2006.

Get involved today! Visit
MorganJamesPublishing.com/giving-back

This book is dedicated to every woman who ever wondered why she couldn't find happiness in the *REAL* moments of life. And to my Grandmothers, who give me hope everyday: Marcia, JoAnn, MaryOlive, and Betty-Jean.

Table of Contents

Foreword

Much like many of my friendships these days, I met Lacy through our shared interest in pornography addiction. She and I both have recovery stories that led us to lead others caught in the chains of compulsive sexuality. Shortly after we met, Lacy generously endorsed my book *Life After Lust* and went on to use it with the women she works with. Now, I have the honor of supporting her by sharing with you why *Addicted to Love* can be a catalyst of major change in your life.

Working as a sexual addiction therapist who guides both female and male addicts through the recovery journey, I know firsthand how rare it is for women struggling with sex, pornography, and love addiction to seek help. I believe the main reason for this is shame. Some of this shame comes from living in a world where sex addiction is advertised as a male issue, strengthening a woman's belief that something must be wrong with her if she struggles in this way. Sadly, when a woman finally admits to struggling with sexual compulsivity, she is socially scolded or met with surprise, deepening her sense of brokenness and isolation.

That is why Lacy's book *Addicted to Love* is such a needed resource for women today. Here, the female addict is not met with rejection but with open arms of acceptance. Not only does Lacy normalize sex and love addiction as struggles women have, but she boldly shares that she's been there too. Lacy knows from experience the wounds women suffer. She has felt that pain. Leading with vulnerability, Lacy shares in this book how she's both struggled and courageously stepped into the light of a new life. All despairing readers will find hope here.

That being said, Lacy doesn't sugar-coat recovery. She tells it like it is, based on her personal recovery and the experiences she's had leading others. Sometimes the truths she shares will sting. As you'll soon see, Lacy doesn't say what women *want* to hear, she says what they *need* to hear. When we are deep in denial, the truth is bitter but beautiful because it is the birthplace of healing. Lacy speaks the uncomfortable truth because she loves you. Her care for her readers is palpable throughout the pages of this book.

Lacy and I share a strong belief in the value of empowerment. Throughout her book, you'll hear encouraging echoes of "You can do this! I believe in you!" When sex and love addiction feel so heavy and hopeless, Lacy's positive voice will propel you forward, inspiring you to fight for your freedom. All of us have self-critical voices, screaming that we will never change. Lacy's message bellows above them, shouting that we should never quit.

Not only is *Addicted to Love* written to inspire but also to equip. This book is not just a pep talk but will also prepare you for the rough and real road ahead. Themes in this book such as Accountability, Gratitude, Courage, and Honesty are not only emphasized as important values but are accompanied with guidance that will help you go deeper, engaging in real-life change.

Are you ready to embark on the adventure of *Addicted to Love*? Lacy and I agree that recovery is difficult, possible, and worth the effort. You and those you love are worth the effort. I can only imagine how many lives will be transformed by the book you now hold in your hands. I sincerely hope that one of them is yours.

Forest Benedict, LMFT, SATP
Author of *Life After Lust*
April 5, 2018
Fresno, CA

Introduction

So many women struggle to keep their hearts and minds free of distraction and fantasy. Trust me, I get how alluring fantasy and distraction can be, especially for those of us who grew up in emotionally neglectful or sexually damaging environments. That's why I wrote this book!

I love Pia Melody's *Facing Love Addiction*, Marnie Ferree's *No Stones*, and so many other great books for female love and relationship addicts. What I am attempting to add to the conversation is an open and clear dialogue on the very real issue of women, romantic fantasy, and all of the other distractions we use to cover up the pain. Even more, early in my own recovery, I wanted a book from a woman who knew what I was going through and who was courageous enough to call us both out. I wanted a bold declaration of "Fantasy is killing your marriage, and that is not love! Neither is what you create in your mind, my dear friend!" These other books touch on it, even explain so well what was happening in our world of fantasy and why. What a relief to hear from these authors that I was not alone, not unique in my struggles, and not to blame. I was responsible, but I was not to blame. That message started my healing. I still needed another woman to take my hand and teach me to love myself into a recovered life. I wanted that life to be free of my inner fantasy world and the other distractions I used to numb the pain of what was happening in reality.

You know the life I mean, don't you? A life of honesty, integrity, and a resolved history. Women like us crave deep, boundaried love, where we feel cherished, seen, and held accountable so we can continue to progress into that perfect Love of God and all mankind. That is the book I could not find, but desperately needed. I needed a book that taught me the difference between helpful, goal-oriented planning and dreaming, and my distracting fantasy world. A book that reassured me fantasy was not helping, even though everyone else seemed to be using it. That is what I want to accomplish with *Addicted to Love*. I want to share the great values-based skills I have learned, while sharing enough of my story to encourage you in the dark, lonely moments. I also want to help you see how common our "addiction" is. Women with trauma, childhood abuse and neglect, women who may have been sexually abused in their marriages, need a safe place where other women can wrap their arms around us and say, "Me, too" as we cry tears of recognition and healing, together.

There is so much power in those two words, no matter what we are talking about. This book is my "me, too." Here, we say "me, too" for so many reasons, some more painful than others, some more shame-filled and destructive. That's okay. Me, too.

This book is about you, as a woman in relationship to men. Some of the relationships are familial, some are friendships, some are co-workers, others are supervisors. You go to church, school, work, the gym, anywhere and everywhere, and run into men. I want to talk about the attractions outside of marriage, though. Those men, who could be any man, intrigue, mystify, and sometimes intentionally lure us in. Those men who unwittingly breed our attractions and romantic feelings because we don't know how to have healthy, platonic, heterosexual friendships. I want to talk about the men we never speak to but carry on deeply intimate fantasy relationships with in our minds. Whatever their station in your life, you know the men I mean. The earlier in life these fantasy relationships began, the earlier your feelings of abandonment and loss opened up. For me, it was first grade. I never *actually* talked to him outside of my head, but he was my "boyfriend" until the end of second grade, when I replaced him with a fifth-grade soccer player (who I also never talked to). These boys would help me with my homework, bring me candy, and talk to me on the playground. Mind you, this was all in my head.

Take a minute to think back to your first fantasy relationship. The specifics of the fantasy are irrelevant. What I want you to focus on is your abandonment and losses before that first imaginary relationship, or your first deep dive into fantasy. What comes up for you when you go back, pull back the fantasy, and look behind it at the pain? What were you and others doing in these fantasies? Maybe you were fifteen and your first boyfriend took off with your best friend. Or maybe you were four and your father left to buy cigarettes and never came back. Whatever it was, your heart knows. As it comes up, I encourage you to talk to a close friend or family member, even a therapist, about the pain and loss. That little girl needs healing, and she will be back throughout our journey together. You will learn to nurture her and give her what she needed, which will steal so much of the power from fantasy. By taking care of that little one inside of you, the woman you are will start to heal. She will start to trust. As she does, you will find yourself running from reality less often.

So, I encourage you to stop and talk with her, journal, even ugly cry when you need to. You know the cry I mean, with streams of tears, snot, and maybe even a few choice words screamed at those who left her to fend for herself, long before she was capable. She will thank you for it, and you will be amazed at what witnessing that for yourself, then speaking the words you needed to hear back then, will do for your heart. Ugly cry is messy, but it is the most beautiful and courageous cry known to any woman. Give yourself space to really cry. Then see the beauty and healing radiate and warm you like sunlight after weeks of storms. Also remember, the best naps come after an ugly cry! Don't try this at work but do try it. The healing is indescribable.

You may also have any form of trauma or abandonment, neglect, or any of the varied abuses from childhood. Maybe your father was absent, emotionally neglectful, or abusive, so you never really learned the ins and outs of heterosexual friendships and communication. Maybe other male role models were inappropriate and acted out their poor boundaries through myriad forms of abuse. It is possible your mother showcased you, led you to believe the young men coming to visit you were actually there for her, or otherwise sabotaged your personal sexual development with comments, bragging, or hurtful glares. Or maybe you felt paraded around, like a living barbie doll for her enjoyment and exhibition. Perhaps you've just always been shy, with or without abuse, so you never really learned to relate in healthy ways. You might still be shy, and play out scenarios in your head, where you have more control over the outcome.

Or maybe your story is a little different. You might be a stay-at-home mom who needs a relaxing hobby to unwind. A friend loaned you a book, and now you seek tantalizing encounters in other books or in your head. They feel good. If only your husband knew how to make you feel this way. Perhaps you've even started flirting with random men here and there. They might be strangers, they might not be. What's the harm? He's just a waiter/store clerk/delivery man you will never see again. He's just a guy at work, it doesn't mean anything. Why not banter back with a sexy play on words or a well-timed innuendo? You'd never actually act on it. Besides, a girl needs a little spice, and the waiter flirted first... There's no harm in looking, is there? What's a little friendly banter with an attractive man? It doesn't *mean* anything, right?

Whatever the reason you struggle to form and maintain healthy, well-boundaried heterosexual friendships or work relationships, there's a good chance the beginning of your struggle had nothing to do with choices you made. It would be a rare story indeed if it was your fault. That's the good news. The bad news is, no matter how much of this is not your fault, it is costing you big time. That cost is your responsibility, and that may not seem fair. As time moves on, though, the cost only increases. It will forever be your responsibility to manage, and I know how unfair that seems. Hang in there, though. The management gets easier, and responsibility does not mean blame.

Your marriage/dating relationship could be in significant danger. If not now, your addictive and compulsive behaviors will at some point start to unravel your intimate partnerships. That must be managed. You may start to feel worse and worse about the situation(s) you are in. You start to double guess your own worth, feeling less and less worthy of the love and respect of those around you, the love you so desperately need. These behaviors and thoughts are toxic, and you may not know how to make them stop. The thoughts are constant and relentless. You have lost control, and don't know if you can ever get it back. Maybe you have considered taking your own life because you can't see any other way out of the insanity. It actually seems like a better idea than coming clean and trying to get help. Besides, who could you ask for help? You feel like you are the only one going through this, and that no one else could possibly understand. If you use pornography compulsively, you may feel even more out of place. Porn is a guy's issue, isn't that what the world would say?

Now, I want you to imagine a new world. It is different than the one you have always known. In this world, you are the typical woman with an active intellect. Just like most of the other women here, you never really learned what it meant to commit. Your heart was on your sleeve, and in vulnerable moments, could be tainted by passing thoughts and harmful sexual energy from the environment. The difference in this world is you no longer wear your heart outside your chest. It is safely where it belongs, available to interact with and feel, but not open to infidelity or impulsive desires. In this world, you truly understand your value, and never compromise it. It is non-negotiable, and you boundary all of your interactions with self-awareness and integrity. You do not need to worry, or even think about other people's boundaries, because you know yours. Those are the boundaries that matter – the ones you keep with and for yourself. Your heart is open, loving, connecting, and it is protected from lustful, wandering, compulsive, and unbridled longings. These longings still float by you, they may even land on your skin, but as soon as you feel them, you send them on their way. You know how to manage yourself, and your relationships show it. Your husband knows he can trust you, and your children feel secure. When you are with them, you can stay in the moment, soaking in every giggle, every punchline, every tear. Nothing has ever felt so real, and you can hardly believe this is your life. The love you feel for these people, for all people, is pure, clean, and nurturing in its rightful ways. There is no fear of being rejected, discovered, abandoned or alone, because you no longer fear reality. You no longer keep secrets. Reality has become the greatest gift you've ever known, and you can scarcely remember the time you spend distracted from it. Even in chaos and turmoil, you feel centered, calm, and in the moment. You know who you are, and value that worth in others. You are a Daughter of God and you are perfectly whole. Life brings what you need, and you embrace it with hope and surrendered courage. This is the perfect moment, and you are alive to witness it. Can you imagine living such a life? It is not as far away as you might think.

Now back to where you may be now. You've known your relationships were off for a long time, but have not been able to break free of these habits. You are fully aware some of your behaviors, and most, if not all, of your fantasies are not appropriate. You keep secrets, hide things, may even live a double life. If it isn't a full-blown double life, it certainly feels like it at times! You worry about your intimate friends and romantic partner finding out or picking up on something being off with you. The secret-keeping is costing you sleep and peace of mind. Relaxing is becoming impossible, and you can't turn off the thoughts in your head. You start Googling things like, "How do I get him out of my head?" "What if I'm not in love with my husband anymore?" and "Is it okay to have a crush on a co-worker?" You are careful, so you clear the browser history or fill it up with other search topics so no one can tell. Maybe you are terrified someone will find out how much you enjoy reading romantic and sexual encounters online. What would they think of you? Good women don't do this kind of thing, especially not at work or during church, right? You wonder if you can even call yourself "good" anymore. The answer is yes. You can still call yourself good. Your past, your thoughts, do not define you, and you can start now to create a future you want. Before long, you will witness it coming to life before your eyes. You were not created to be perfect now; you were created to work toward perfection. The original definition of perfection is "whole." And you *are* whole. You are flawed, you are human, and just like everyone else on Earth, you are whole. You can choose. It isn't always easy, but it gets easier. You must have faith and start walking into the darkness though, or the fear will paralyze you.

Now, I want to talk about affairs and the word "addiction" for a few minutes. We also need to talk about how you use the word "love." I get that mainstream psychology and media call what we do "love addiction." Your drug of choice may not be exactly the same as another woman's, or even mine. I don't like the phrase "love addiction" because I feel it glamorizes using another human being to distract us or make us feel better through a dopamine or oxytocin hit. We are not in love with our targets (the men we become infatuated with, or convince ourselves we are in love with), we are using them. With that clarification, we will expand, then replace this definition. We will include any heart, relationship, romance, or sex-based compulsive behavior or obsessive thoughts. I have chosen this approach because what we are truly seeking is love. We *need* deeply connected, honest, vulnerable, safe, loving relationships. We are seeking loving relationships, by using chaos and intensity instead of integrity and real connection. First of all, an imaginary relationship in your mind is not, and never can be, love. You need to stop using that word to describe it. "Fantasy" or "relationship addiction" are more accurate. Even then, I struggle to call them addictions, because what we are doing we do to cover up the pain of abuse and neglect, even if it is self-neglect. For these reasons, I refer to these internal workings as "distractions," and the external behaviors "compulsions." I may use the word "addiction" here and there, because these distractions are certainly intoxicating. You probably know how just thinking about a target can make everything else go away, thus "distraction." You also know how it take a team of WWF wrestlers to hold you back from sending that email, text message, or re-reading them multiple times. Sweetie, we call that compulsive behavior. It might border on obsession.

I've learned that the female sex, love, pornography, fantasy, romance, and relationship junkies have much more in common with each other than they do with the men who identify with the exact same compulsive grouping. This book is for women with compulsive love/sex-based relationship patterns and behaviors.

Now, I'm going to use a big word here, but I know you are ready for it. If you feel like throwing this book at the wall, that's cool. Pick it back up when you are ready. Here we go. Anything that pulls you away from your marriage emotionally, sexually, romantically, or in any significant form of distraction, is a type of affair. This goes for romance novels (even teen romance), pornography, self-stimulation (masturbation), flirting, or anything else that replaces the very real man and other people in your life in any way.

Well, crap, right? I know. This was a dirty trick. Sorry. Well, not totally, because I care about you and your happiness, and I also know it stings. For me, I really enjoyed my teen drama anime. Poor boyfriends – I only had them because I needed to feel wanted. That was the one thing anime couldn't give me. Ouch! And yes, I'm absolutely calling out sexy fanfiction, romantic fiction, and tantalizing movies. Hey, I gave up my movie star fantasies. It was hard, but romantic comedy is no longer part of my life. I missed it at first, now I have no taste for it. It's only tempting when a certain actor (who shall remain nameless) comes out with a new one. But it passes fast. Did I have an affair with Mr. Nameless Actor? Not a "real" one, but when I felt intense pain, I'd take off in my head with him. The fact that we need to ask ourselves that question is a good indication we know we have crossed a line. Have the courage to own it. You'll be surprised how much power it gives you to create the life you want. And know this: I will never ask you to do something I would not do. Chances are, I've done it myself and insisted my clients do it, so feel confident that it will help you as well.

Non-physical affairs are even more of an issue with real people. If it is all in your mind, it is a romantic or sexual affair, depending on the content. Because sex was always so scary to me, my fantasy relationships were often of talking, holding hands, and sharing emotional intimacy that never went beyond PG. I didn't want the manipulation sex represented to me. As a young girl, I equated sex with being taken advantage of, being manipulated, not having a choice. As a teen, then even more as an adult, the fantasies were usually non-sexual. I needed control and learned as a very young child how much control I had in my mind. If anything was too upsetting to face, I was in my fantasy world, where Strawberry Shortcake was my best friend and Little Boy Blueberry had a crush on me. He would bring me baskets of berries and we would ride My Little Ponies together. It was necessary back then. Now I see LBB taking care of me as a fill in for the father who left and never came back. Abandonment does crazy things to a child's brain. Those wounds don't heal easily, but they do heal. The first step is to stop living inside a fantasy world.

As adults, you and I both have the strength and responsibility to face reality head on, calling others out on bad behavior and holding them accountable. This goes for physical touch and any other way a fantasy-based affair might pop out of your head. If that conversation went beyond what another highly responsible professional would deem appropriate, or brought up romantic or sexual feelings in you, it crossed a line. It does not matter what did or did not happen for the other person. They can lie, pretend, and may even be in their own forms of denial (which they usually are), but that's not ours to deal with. Even Little Boy Blueberry would be a distraction-based romantic affair for me now. If I relate a man I am attracted to in the real world to my Little Boy Blueberry, I have crossed an emotional line in my head. LBB will always be a part of me, but he is not real, and he is not helping anymore. He has no place in my life, other than as a childhood coping mechanism I'm grateful I had but should not have needed. He covered up pain that has been fully dealt with. He is not real.

REAL Love Recovery

You might be wondering why I use "real" in all caps a few times in this book and on my website. In recovery, we often give ourselves ultimatums (stop it!) and hold a perfectionistic standard for ourselves (stop that, too!). I created REAL to give you just a few things to focus on right away. "REAL" stands for Responsible, Empowered, Accountable, and Languaged. These four pillars of recovery, if you will, can make the first few months go much better. You will build on them, add to them, color them for your life (without excuses or justification!) and make them your own.

You do this by taking responsibility for yourself. Yes, emotions come in faster than we can catch them sometimes. And we get to learn to manage them. This is our responsibility. As you know, emotions cannot be controlled, but you certainly do have what it takes to handle them responsibly. Your actions and thoughts are the same thing. You can learn to manage how long an emotion or thought stays and can become a rock star at managing your behaviors.

Empowerment is a big part of learning that management and control, for yourself and others. Have you noticed how I keep telling you that you can do this, and that you have what it takes? Girlfriend, that's me empowering you! If you choose to believe me then to trust yourself, that is you empowering yourself! So cool. Once you have learned to empower yourself to choose, speak up, and act for yourself, you have seriously mastered a good third of this program. Empowerment and honesty are the cement that holds your recovery foundation together. It's even more awesome as you learn to empower others to be honest with you, to speak up, and to take responsibility for themselves.

While I love all of the values in this program, it is empowerment that is missing from so many other programs, especially sex and addiction recovery programs written by men. Bless their hearts, men just do not get how women must learn personal empowerment. As women, we are taught that if we are strong, we are too much – or worse, a nasty "B word." It has been a man's world for so long, few of us even noticed what was missing. Empowerment is what will give you the courage to do what needs to be done for protection of yourself, your family, your heart, and your future. Get some.

Accountability is the most vulnerable value we will discuss. You need other women you can call on for a pep talk, a responsible conversation, and to help you see your part in the unhealthy dynamics of every-day interactions. Finding a few women you can call on empowers you to choose connection over addiction and compulsive isolation. It also teaches you to face the fears that have kept you isolated emotionally. It can feel scary, but after practicing it becomes second nature, much like the emotional hide and seek game became part of your coping skills early on.

Finally comes language. There is not a chapter on language, but it's pretty easy to understand. This is where you put what you think, feel, do, experienced, and survived into words. "Language it!" Now, I said easy, but I am very aware it is also extremely difficult to get used to. That doesn't even take into account how painful language can be. For traumatic experiences, especially around sexual abuse or assault, I highly recommend a therapist who is skilled in validation, compassion, and trauma recovery. If you need one, I can recommend a couple; contact me. It is best, however, that you find your own. She needs to mesh with you, and mine are pretty brassy. Then again, you are still reading this book, so maybe brassy works for you! A good therapist will never blame you for abuse, and will help you let go through self-empowerment, which also means taking responsibility for how you let things impact your life now. She will always hold you accountable but knows how to do so gently and with compassion.

Do you see why "language" is not part of this book? It's not even part of my beginning program, because you really do need to take care of trauma with someone who is trained and licensed. That's not to say you cannot still read this book, and work this program, even in my REAL Love Recovery groups. I just want you to have that extra support when you need it!

That's a lot of information, and I totally understand that you might be a little nervous. If you are full-on terrified, that is normal on so many levels! Don't worry, we are going to build a great foundation together. You already have what it takes, now I will teach you to *do* what it takes.

A Note on Fear

Many women in recovery face the fear and worry of "who am I now?" This might manifest in different ways. It can be hard to know who we are or will become without being who we have always been. The fear will hold you back, though. I'm asking you right now to face the fear of failing, of not being perfect at this journey, of making mistakes. Face the fear of not knowing, then choose to trust the process. I'll tell you right now, you are going to screw this up. A lot! You will fail, miserably. And I promise you, that wholeness will never mean perfect in this lifetime. Right now, you are messy, bleeding, and afraid of one more program failing to fix you. I get it. There's not a lot out there for women like us, and it sucks! What if you don't find good support, or your family won't forgive you? What if you decide you really, truly want to save your marriage, and it is too late? I don't have all those answers. I do know you have the strength to do this because you have been doing it. Maybe not *well,* but you have been pressing forward. The fact that you are still trying is proof you have determination. You can get far on determination. You can get further with a good roadmap. Let me lay out the map, you just worry about staying calm and not going all perfectionist on me. Perfectionism will sabotage your new life faster than anything else.

As you read through this book, I'd like you to do so all at once, stopping for the exercises as you feel ready, but in order. It would be fabulous if you did so in two weeks or so. Then, I want you to relax. Just getting this information in your head, bringing it to your awareness, is going to cause a change in you. You will not be the same person two weeks later, even if you stop there. You will be better. There is so much more for you, though, so I want you to then read it again. This time, no skipping anything you haven't already done as part of reading this book. Do all of the exercises. Stop and take time with your thoughts, as I have that time built into the book. Reflect, journal, talk to someone you trust. Determine what else you need to do to fully apply any particular value to your own life. Make the chapters and concepts yours. Soak them in, hate them, cry, fall in love with them, and above all, *practice* them. Love yourself enough to give yourself a new way of living, breathing, and loving others. Do this for others in your life, but mostly for that courageous woman in the mirror.

This book is a compilation of the best recovery tools, healing behaviors, and skills I have found. Few have come from books or programs written for women dealing with unbridled hearts. It doesn't matter – the techniques are timeless, common knowledge, and effective. Many of us just missed the lessons on how to use them. They work. That is what counts. These strategies are taken from multiple fields of research, my time studying psychology, and personal experience. You will not be guided through a "program," you will be shown a roadmap of values that will help you heal your heart and find peace. Hopefully that means happiness and love in your closest relationships. Even if not, you will still be able to breathe deeply knowing you have changed. These are the very values I base my own recovery on, and they have helped my coaching clients, group participants, and family to come into full integrity in all areas of life.

You will be asked to make changes and record your thoughts. You will also take an inventory of your experiences, choices, triggers and acting in behaviors. They are called "acting in" behaviors because they focus inward and involve only you. Women like us invalidate and cut ourselves down with every decision we make. We beat ourselves up and treat ourselves worse than we'd ever let anyone treat our closest friends. That's about to change. You will learn these basic values, get suggestions for activating them in your life, and be encouraged to live them fully. I will push you, stretch you, call you out, and I will love you. You will have the opportunity to build your own plan moving forward, based on these values and the principles of an empowered, responsible life that they rest upon. Only you can make this work, and I am grateful to be able to share the journey with you.

Keep hope, and never stop moving!

My Story

You may be wondering who I think I am to talk about female fantasy and emotional distraction like an expert. Sure, I research this stuff, and love gathering data. As with most passionate research buffs, however, I do also have skin in the game. My skin is my own story of fantasy and distraction from a young age. In fact, my preschool teacher commented on it for my first report card. "Lacy is a delight to have in class. She does get distracted often and is always in her own world."

It didn't get better. Every grade school teacher reported the same thing in my permanent records, which used to come home, hand-written and photo copied every school year. Some teachers and students were nicer than others. I earned my "Spacey Lacy" nickname fairly by first grade.

Before first grade was kind of a blur. I had a sweet little best friend that year who had somewhat the same issue I did with daydreaming. We used to sit or stand anywhere we could get privacy and talk about our daydreams. I felt like I had found my soul mate. She thought about the same stuff I did! And we fed each other's fantasy with new ideas. What our "real" families were like, where we lived. We designed dresses together, and dream bedrooms with all the toys we saw our friends have. We dreamed together about our teacher liking us and being so proud we were able to finish our classwork on time. We laughed about the kids that wouldn't play with us tripping or running in to each other and crying. By third grade, I was being mercilessly teased by "Rusty Buckets Jerk-Face Dusty" for wearing dirty clothes or not having underwear on (how could he tell?) I was sure he had X-ray vision, so I started wearing my brother's or sister's underwear if I didn't have any clean. No one helped me when I cried about his teasing, and no compassion was available at home. My mother did teach me to do my own laundry, though, and that helped – when I remembered. I was so thankful to have my fantasy world to escape into whenever I needed. No one teased me there, and I had pretty clothes. My mom wasn't depressed my dad didn't move away to have a better family without me, and my step-dad kept his hands to himself. He was just a nice dad who loved me as much as he loved my little sister. You know, enough to not hurt me anymore, with belts, words, or anything else.

In sixth grade, we moved to a new city, and my anxiety shot through the roof. I became suicidal, tried to run away multiple times, and ended up figuring out boys liked me back. Even some of the cute ones wanted to talk to me! I would have multiple "boyfriends," who all happened to also be best friends and hang out together. I'd date one of them by sitting next to him when we all chatted on the stairs or caught locusts. Then we would break up, and I'd start "dating" whomever else. It was all innocent and adorably naïve. It felt so good to feel loved and seen. I was on cloud nine and had no shortage of attention from these young men. That's when I learned the power of flirting and female wiles. I was twelve.

We moved to a new school and neighborhood just a few months later. I was an avid D.A.R.E. student, rising to the top of my class at my old school. (D.A.R.E. stands for Drug and Alcohol Resistance Education, just in case you didn't grow up in the 80s and 90s). That taught me that teachers give attention and praise to the students who serve and don't do drugs, so I rose to the top again, and was eventually asked to mentor other kids to stay away from drugs, alcohol, and gangs. I was a "good girl" and got a great deal of attention from the teachers and the officers involved. The attention from adults was manna from heaven through high school. Every club that needed an officer, I joined. I kept busy, felt needed and loved, and came to know many people at school. I was thankful to have my own life away from the pain and loneliness at home.

Then there was Kyle. For whatever reason, his family lived with ours for a few months. Kyle was two years older than I was, and I thought he was *so* cute! Then he started blocking me in the hallway and asking why I wouldn't kiss him, putting his hands on my waist. I could smell his gum. I was 12, maybe 13 years old at this point, and not at all interested in kissing him or doing anything else he talked about (ahem, "doing *it*"). I just wanted to marry him! He scared the life out of me, but thankfully never did any actual harm. It blows my mind I had such a thing for him when he also scared me so badly. Aside from an overly sexualized sense of humor, nothing more happened. I add this in because it illustrates how afraid of boys and men I actually was, and how it fed into my need for safe romantic, non-sexual encounters. It also woke in me that desire to affect the boys (later, men), around me. That power is intoxicating. My fantasy world became the only place I was safe, and I was constantly trying to live there, with "safe" versions of the boys I liked. I'd venture out in less threatening places to get my hit of "real love." I'd flirt, "date" a guy for a few weeks, then crawl back into my internal world. Crazy-making. I see that now, but it seemed totally harmless back then. Good grief, I never even kissed a guy until well after turning sixteen, and wasn't a huge fan afterward. Fantasy had so much more power with no risk. I was in control inside my mind.

At thirteen, I babysat for a couple who had enough pornography accessible to satiate just about anyone. I was told the movies were off limits, so I didn't go near them. Then I found a magazine the size of a TV guide as I was house cleaning for them. There were a few pictures, which grossed me out, and many more stories of sexual encounters. I became so enthralled, many weekends I'd watch the kids for free so I could read for hours after putting them to bed. I was in heaven. These stories were all I needed to enter my fantasy world now. They were so much more intoxicating.

I continued acting in through high school. No more babysitting, but that was fine. There was more than enough in my head to last a lifetime. However, I'd watch sexy teen anime – we called it "Bubble gum" back then. That escalated into more overtly sexualized genres, and I always imagined I was the cute girl everyone wanted. The boys would all be in love with me, and I would watch the romance unfold … safely. Until recently, I had been puzzled that these fantasies were never about real relationships, but always make believe. Now I see that for what it was: an escape from reality, a place where I was in control and safe, and it took care of the rest of my loneliness. The pain of my father having a new family, one he loved, didn't exist, because I had these boys. I didn't need him, and it didn't hurt that he didn't want me. My boyfriends were my excuse for liking anime, and my surrogates. They took care of me. It started with "clean" stories, which quickly became more and more sexualized. I felt like a freak for liking it (don't only boys like porn?), but the truth is, I was always glad when someone brought it, and that the adults in the house were okay with it. They'd even join in watching or rent it for us. Now I see that as insane. Back then, we were the cool house.

I was also active in a church community, so the confusion was insurmountable. I learned to compartmentalize and not bring the two groups of friends up with each other. I needed them both to stay alive (literally, I was often suicidal), as I didn't really fit in with the girls at church. Trouble is, I didn't know it until adulthood. No wonder I lived a double life! It sucked to not feel I fit anywhere, and teenaged girls are a poor substitute for a loving home. Teen boys can never fill the hole of losing a father. They just didn't have the skills or life experience I needed.

By fifteen, my eating disorder was out of control. I put all of my energy into looking like the anime girls did in miniskirts and the little black dresses my mother and I would share when we went to live-action role-plays. I would play a seductive, beautiful art curator who happened to be a 125-year-old vampire. Talk about living out my inner world! "Rima Dalv" gave me a way to interact with all the attractive men (whatever their age), safely. (I wasn't me, for shame! I'd never do that! Rima is just a tease. I must play my part…) At one party, which for some reason lacked adults, only us teens were there – and so was the beer. I never drank it because those "you might get drugged" lessons had sunk in well. My crush, DJ, did though. I had been trying to get his attention for a while. We ran around the house, him chasing, me letting him catch up, but heaven forbid I let him kiss me. He told me he was in love with me, had been forever, he was just too chicken to admit it sober. He knew I was just scared, "C'mon, let's just give it a try." He was right, I was totally into him. But this was not the life I wanted. Teen alcohol and sex, parties without parents and turning away from the values I had picked up from church, and really *did* want to learn to live? My life changed that night, as I realized the road I was on. I stepped away, told him I'd see him later, and had a sober friend take me home. That was the most painful walk-away of my life. I literally had to leave a part of me behind so I could move forward. No more parties, no more of this messy romantic drama. No more DJ. I didn't want to hurt anyone else. I truly cared about him but did not want to join him in his world, as Rima Dalv or anyone else. I didn't want this to be my world anymore. It was my playground, and my worst nightmare. I couldn't go back.

This group was from an online community, like Facebook, but in Ascii. If you don't know what that is, look it up for a good laugh. Facebook was to Ascii chatrooms what cell phones are to pagers. Good times were had by all, but only in multi colored fonts. Y'all, we created LOL and ROTFLMBO. We also created /passionate kiss and /w want to chat alone? (for private chat, a.k.a. "whisper"). I'd spend hours and hours having conversations, flirting, teasing, and otherwise distracting myself from real life. I could get the sexual rush without having to worry about someone wanting follow through. It was ridiculous. Most of my boyfriends and romantic interests from fifteen to seventeen came from here. I became less involved in the real world for a few years. It wasn't until college, and not having a computer when I moved, that I was able to break free. This was in the mid-90s, before things were so visually appealing. Thinking about what kids grow up with now, blows my mind! My experiences have led to serious boundaries around social media in our house. Hopefully the kids will thank me someday. If not, I'm okay with that.

Want to know the most insane part? I would have random guys I didn't know pick me up to go to the weekly meet-ups or parties mutual "friends" were having. It's a miracle I survived, coming out relatively unharmed. Even just a year after quitting the insanity, I realized how close I came to be just another missing teen girl. I was absolutely being watched over by unseen angels.

I cleaned up quite a bit in college and started taking life more seriously. I did notice, however, that being attractive and having a '59 VW bug got me a *lot* of attention from the guys in class. And I had no problem trading them free work on my car for dinner! I was so good, I even got them to pay for dinner half the time. It makes me cringe now. If I ever run into the young man who worked on my car so much that his family thought we *were* dating, I probably owe him a lot of money – and a serious apology. Sorry, Danny! I dated a lot, but I rarely even talked to the guys I was actually attracted too. They terrified me. I convinced myself these other guys were safe, because if I didn't want to actually date them, there was no danger. I didn't say it made sense.

Then at nineteen I met and became engaged to a man I truly fell in love with. The world changed, and I realized I was worthy of so much more. So much shifted, and I stopped treating myself like a cheap commodity. We would sit outside his apartment for hours, just talking in the Vegas summer nights. The only conversations I had about football that I ever enjoyed were with him. It didn't matter what we talked about, just as long as he kept talking. It was when he asked me to marry him with an emerald ring, custom made, with white-gold leaves, just like we talked about, that I could imagine myself happy forever. I used to say I had never seen eternity except when I looked in his eyes. For reasons I can only guess at, we did not get married. His roommates teased me that only a gay guy could refuse me, but it didn't stop the tears or mend the broken heart. He left for the Navy days after we broke up. Said he couldn't stand Vegas without me but couldn't ruin my life by marrying me. I still don't fully know why, but we both knew we were not meant to be together. I can see some of the issues we had, years later. It was good for both of us that we parted ways. I only hope he has found whatever he was looking for.

Then I met Jon. He was athletic, funny, and could not seem to get enough time with me. We went to plays, on picnics, roller blading, and danced like crazy people every chance we got. I loved the attention, the way Jon took care of things, and how he was able to handle my complicated emotional states (which were many). He even volunteered to take me to Washington, DC, where my former fiancé would be singing the national anthem for the President of the United States. Then my ex found out that Jon wanted to marry me, and he never called back. Cell phones weren't a thing. I found out later that he told Jon to take care of me for both of them, and to help me move on. He wouldn't be contacting me again, because it was best for us both. Boy, was I angry! But Jon kept his word. We got married and have been together for over 20 years now. Jon has been an attentive, loving, wonderful husband. We have a relationship that nurtures us both.

I feel extremely blessed. There have been challenges, many of which came from us both having poor and undefined sex-based boundaries. Thankfully, we have moved past the really hard stuff and into a relationship of mutual respect, cherished regard, and incredible trust.

I do need to make a note here. We have come so far, but it is only because he is a humble, responsible man, and forgiveness is my superpower. Actually, we both have that superpower. It works quite well in marriage. We are just careful to not use it to cover up hurt feelings anymore! That was a challenge for a long time. We have both made major mistakes and hurt each other deeply. To some extent, I think that is just marriage, or any important, close relationship. We have boundaries in place that one or both of us must be reminded of occasionally. We took a long, painful walk into marital sex abuse that about ended us, but we are good now. He was never taught about sexual respect or boundaries, and neither was I. I certainly never learned I could have boundaries, let alone enforce them. Thankfully, we both learned. The increased safety in our marriage as he has learned to manage himself, coupled with my work on my romantic fantasy and "love" addiction, has brought us to a place I never thought possible. Forgiveness is nearly complete, on both of our sides. We both married an addict, and of course, we married our perfect addicted match-up. I was addicted to what I could create in my head, and he was hooked on me. He classifies himself as a marital lust addict in recovery. Sadly, for us both, I was his drug for a very long time. He still struggles to forgive himself fully, which I can understand. It has been hard for me to forgive myself for staying distracted while my life went on around me. We made memories, I loved my children the best I knew how, but a part of my heart was always inaccessible to them. That is my biggest regret. Because I know I will need their forgiveness someday, it makes it easier to forgive the hurts I have endured. Plus, I know that I am a whole human being, and that no matter what has happened, I can live a full, happy, and beautiful life. The past does not define me. It does not need to define our marriage either. I've even forgiven myself for not knowing, doing, or believing better. If anyone deserves compassion and love, it is the lost little girl who was never given the chance to have a boundary, and never learned how lovable or valuable she was.

I want to make a special mention here. At twelve, I met a young woman whose family took me in as their own. I have since been legally adopted by and become a member of that family. The little girl inside me has a safe, secure, loving home, with parents that have made up for all that was missed. That young woman I mentioned is now my adopted "Irish twin," as we share a birth year. Her sister, who is now also my "big" sister (by ten months!) became my best friend in high school, and is now our children's godmother. The family that got me through is now mine permanently. The mom I used to pretend was mine, who sent me half-frozen muffins because she knew I wasn't eating, is now my mom in every sense of the word. I would not have written this book, found the courage to heal my marriage and family, and become a voice for other women, without her and Dad. Mom and Dad, thank you for finding me. I will never be able to return what you have given me, and thankfully I have forever to keep trying. What a gift to have our sacred contract fulfilled!

Chapter
2

The Road Map

"Alice asked the Cheshire Cat, who was sitting in a tree,
'What road do I take?'
The cat asked, 'Where do you want to go?'
'I don't know,' Alice answered.
'Then,' said the cat, 'it really doesn't matter, does it?'"

– Lewis Carroll, Alice's Adventures in Wonderland

I have compiled the habits that finally brought me out of my distracted life and into the beautiful life I had all along. They are called "values" in this book, as they are more than habits or steps. These are changes in how we view and interact with the world. You will have the opportunity to dig deep into your behaviors and root out the damaged parts of yourself, replacing them with healthy skills that work.

Admitting to the problem is critical. Committing to the work is necessary. Learning new ways of being will help fill the void left by the absence of the destructive patterns. These are more than suggestions, they are character traits that will change the way you do everything. They are also not "steps" along a path, but new ways of interacting with the world around you. You will decide how to best incorporate them into your life. I will only shine the light on the jewels, urging you to pick them up.

Some of these values will feel familiar, others will not. Many will be concepts you have heard but are presented in a new light here. Using them in the ways suggested may feel awkward or like an ill-fitting pair of shoes at first. If you just hang in there and keep practicing, they will start to feel more comfortable. It took twenty, thirty, forty, sixty or more years to get where you are now. You've learned habits and coping skills along the way that are deeply ingrained. These will take time to change out for the new and improved skill sets now available to you.

I have broken the process into eight key values, as mentioned. Each value builds on the ones before, and feeds into those that come after. For example, you will work on honesty before you work on taking responsibility for your actions and the state of your life. But before you work on honesty, you will work on accountability and courage. These skills will help you prepare for the inevitable triggers of life. Previously, these triggers sent you into fantasy, erotic literature, or some other form of sex-based distraction. Now you will learn to manage these triggers with integrity.

A word of caution: withdrawal from any behaviors or habitual thought patterns mentioned at any point in this book is very real. You may feel extra fatigued, moody, anxious, hungry, vulnerable, shaky, or even like you have the flu. Basically, if you feel like you have the flu, or are losing your mind, it just might be withdrawals. Yours may be more or less severe, depending on length of time and depth of distracting habits. You will crave your drug of choice (ahem, interactions with a target) as if it were a physical drug. We will call these compulsive drives. They can be strong, but you are stronger. They rarely last long (from a few minutes to a few hours), and once you get through them, they begin to space further and further apart, eventually becoming less intense or stopping altogether.

So, as you read this book, if you feel especially drawn to one concept over another, go ahead and read it. Spend time with a few things you feel ready for, then circle back. While it is important to understand how the values build on and support each other, it is more important that you maintain movement in the early stages of change, and move in places you are ready to move in. The values will fall into place, just do not neglect to give them each the attention they need.

Our eight values:

1. Accountability
2. Inventory
3. Empowerment through Courage

4. Honesty
5. Here and Now
6. Personal Responsibility
7. Sacrifice and Service
8. Gratitude

Let me give you a brief overview of each value, so you have an idea of where we are headed together.

Accountability

Accountability is the act of reporting how things are going, honestly. There is a great deal of shame around many of the things you do or have done. An accountability partner acts as a safe place to pull out those embarrassing parts of life and share them. Fear of rejection suffocates hope, leaving all it touches without the light needed for change. By sharing these thoughts, feelings, beliefs and behaviors with a trustworthy woman in your life, you can re-evaluate them and see them more clearly. By being accountable for what is happening in the present, you can stop stockpiling mistakes and start to wipe them out as you go along. This will also help you decrease negative behaviors because you know you will need to report them.

Inventory

An investigative inventory gives an overview of what you have done, where you have been, and what events have impacted your life. While I do not encourage deep investigations into past abuse without the support of a responsible, well-trained therapist, knowing those events are there helps. By doing an inventory, you will be able to see patterns, seek validation to move forward, and find your part in your own history. It will also help you understand things you have done well in the past that may offer valuable tools for your current journey. For example, I never knew my upbringing wasn't "normal" until adulthood. Looking back though, I see what a determined, resilient child I was. Seeing those traits from a young age made them more available to me in my present life. Without the inventory of my strengths, I may have missed the fact that I carried those skills all along.

Empowerment

Making empowered choices for yourself, then empowering others to do the same, brings you to a new level of relationship. With empowered choices, you can think more clearly, make better decisions, and find more lasting peace in the events you helped to create. There is no place for blame in a recovered life. Taking responsibility feeds empowerment, leaving us with more options in the long run. It also takes courage, which, when used, increases feelings of empowerment. Good stuff!

Honesty

Honesty is imperative for real movement in any area. It makes the future a great deal easier to face, because there is less to cover up and keep track of. Worry about clean-up later; right now, just begin by working to stay honest moving forward. If those around you know you can be trusted to speak and report only truth, change will be easier for you to make, and them to accept.

Here and Now

Learning to live in the here and now can be especially challenging in the beginning. We get used to letting ourselves be distracted when uncomfortable emotions set it, when what we need to do is stay connected to the moment and learn from it. Why is it uncomfortable? What are you worried about, upset by, or hiding from? By confronting the answers to these questions, you can start to unravel the reasons for needing the distraction and learn to kick them out of your life.

Responsibility

Responsibility is one of the final values for a good reason. It can be deeply terrifying. Realizing you are fully responsible for your part in the past, and in the creation of the present and future can be overwhelming. It is also at the root of empowered decision making. Taking responsibility used to scare me. Now, I see it as a chance to invite another person to see how human I can be. Most people respond well to full personal responsibility. Those who take this type of responsibility never have to worry about what might catch up to them, because they already know how to handle it: with the truth and in humble confession.

Sacrifice, Service, and Gratitude

Making sacrifices, then serving others, takes the focus off ourselves and opens our hearts to those around us. This feeds directly into gratitude. Gratitude is often overlooked in trying to change habits. I'll tell you though, it truly helps. By experiencing, staying with, and expressing gratitude, our hearts start to see more beauty around us. What you focus on will become your reality, like holding a small pebble up close to your eye becomes all you can see. Full expressions of gratitude include service to others as well.

Accountability

*The one we are first and foremost
accountable to is ourselves.*

I'm so excited to take this journey with you! As we talk about accountability, I hope you will think of others who can also join you. We will discuss the kinds of women you need and how to hold yourself accountable in the process of being accountable to others. Accountability is critical in all relationships and endeavors, if we are to live at peace. It might sound a little scary, and that is totally understandable. I'm asking you to be vulnerable.

Did you know "vulnerable" is a four-letter word for many people? It is. We spell it, R-I-S-K, and it can be terrifying! When my therapist insisted I would not heal until I learned to risk through vulnerability, I was more than grumpy. There is a good chance I told her how unhappy I was. In fact, I almost quit therapy! Bleh, vulnerability was not my favorite thing. I still don't love it, but I'm telling you, she was right. Well-placed vulnerability is so healing! It is supposed to feel a little foreign, even frightening at first as you learn to be accountable, experiencing that vulnerable honesty about what is going on for you, and where you are struggling. If it feels hard and you want to run and hide, excellent! That means you are getting to the good stuff and doing the hard work needed to live life fully. You can do it! And I'm right here, cheering you on. Take a minute and think about how committed you are to this process and leaning into your fears. If you are ready, your commitment will carry you through the challenges ahead. If you aren't, think about why, and what you need to do for your future mental, emotional, and sexual health in your relationships.

Being accountable for acting out (with others) or acting in (by ourselves) is important. In many programs, sponsorships are part of recovery. Here, we have online women's groups, which you may already be a part of. If you aren't, not to worry. You just need a close family member or friend you can report to, even just through a simple daily text early on. They don't need to donate hours and hours of their time, and you don't need to bare your soul. Think about who you have in your life that may be a positive accountability partner. Also, this cannot and must not be your husband. No way. He does not need this, he needs to know how you are progressing and see changes for good. Telling him every little lapse in judgment is going to drive him bonkers! For his sake, pick someone else. Eventually, you will learn to be fully personally aware and accountable. At that point, you will only be lapsing rarely, hopefully not relapsing at all. Then he can become an accountability partner. Save your marriage, and don't have him do this until you have serious recovery.

Furthermore, you need to learn to be honest in your accountability to yourself and others. Honesty is covered in-depth in another chapter, so I'm not going into it too much right now. Just know, without it, you'll struggle to get to what keeps you stuck. Accountability will come in a number of ways. We need to be accountable to people, for our behaviors, fantasy, and other habits that are not in alignment with a recovered life. We also get to learn to account for not managing our environment and triggers (i.e. emotions). These things are our responsibility, and it will help to talk about them and find the patterns.

Being accountable for our compulsions and how we manage them can help us find triggers we may not have recognized sooner. I like to keep tally marks on the back of my hand for whatever I am tracking. It gives me time to pause and helps me report to my accountability partner later. This works for triggers, though at this point I recommend you use it to count only the compulsive thoughts. You need a baseline count to understand how many times a day you get sidetracked into obsessive thoughts. How will you track these distractions this week to gain a baseline? After all, our thoughts eventually become our actions, so catching them now can save heartache later. Ultimately, the compulsions we obsess over are not what we really want, so meeting them head-on moves us in the right direction. Once we get space from the behaviors and our "drugs," if you will, the compulsion dies down and we can see this more clearly. Then we can sort out the triggers a little easier. For now, though it may be hard, just trust me. When the compulsive thoughts flare up, reporting to a support person helps identify what might have triggered them so they can be addressed more easily and rapidly.

Lapses (crossing a bottom line put in place to keep us from relapse) and relapses (acting in or acting out with one of our compulsive behaviors) should also be reported. A woman truly seeking a recovered life is also willing to discuss what led to the relapse, identify her part (because we are always responsible for our lapses and our relapses), and plan to do better in the future.

When we cross our own boundaries in any form of intimacy, or allow someone else to cross them, that needs to be discussed as well. You will learn a little about the varied forms of intimacy in the chapter on inventories. By discussing boundary issues, we learn to tighten up, see the need for new or adjusted boundaries, and can get valuable ideas from someone else. A friend once told me that believing what I think just because I think it is dangerous. Now I'm telling you, this is why we check these things out with others! As a coach, I have my clients keep a log for a few weeks, then report at each session. Usually a daily log coupled with a few minutes of personal introspection and meditation before we get too tired in the evening will bring most things back to our attention.

As trauma and abuses come up, I'll usually encourage my coaching clients to find a good therapist. I'll absolutely still work with women who need to work through historical trauma, I just don't specialize in trauma healing or past experience. My work is done in the present with minor jaunts into the past. I find it best to ask close friends and family who have a good therapist for a referral. With a client's permission and the therapist's approval, she and I can even collaborate our efforts to assist you if needed. These kinds of things can be talked about with your accountability support, though they will most likely not be skilled in processing a lot of it. Trust your gut and do what feels right for you. If I ever feel the need is outside my expertise, I'll always be honest. Anyone else who supports you should be as well.

Self-care is, perhaps, the most important skill you can learn. I have seen many (perhaps most) recovery programs not give self-care enough attention, if it is addressed at all. Perhaps the fear is going overboard, but we can learn to manage this with everything else. It is so critical we not overbook ourselves or become obsessed with recovery work. Even recovery work can become a distraction from the day-to-day needs of self and family. You will learn your limits and begin to understand how much you can handle. Early on, I like to recommend cutting out as much as possible the unnecessary running around, so your emotional energy is available for the mental recovery work you are doing. Balance in all things is key. Recovery work needs to be a priority, and it cannot be your whole life. What can you let go of to clear space for quiet time and recovery?

When you check in with your accountability support, be honest about your self-care. What are you doing to recharge? How is your sleep? Are you taking breaks to have fun and build relationships? Above all, what are you doing to build yourself as a person and maintain the vital value of hope? If you want more on self-care, keep an eye on HerRecoveryRoadmap.com, as I'll be adding loads of supplemental materials. By the time this book is released, my new group coaching program will be up, along with a simple recovery tracker, and some other goodies. For now, what self-care steps will you take this week? Put it in your schedule.

The Women

I promised to talk about the kinds of women you will need to support you. These women are highly valuable, and not always easy to find. When I first started recovery, the only woman I had was my therapist … and I *paid* her to be my friend! I'm sure you have one or two women in your life that will fit. These women are kind, compassionate, validating, and honest. They are not afraid to get in your face, tell you the truth, and call you out on your excuses. They love you at your best and honor you at your worst. A friend like this loves you enough to give you the truth as she sees it, straight from the heart, without beating around the bush. And she always does it with love. It is up to you to take the information, find the gems, and not get your feelings hurt by her honesty. That's not to say you need to put up with being ripped apart. It's quite the opposite. She may rip the bandage off quickly, but always has antibiotic ointment and a cleansing cloth in her back pocket. You will be accountable to her through your journey, checking in frequently. Having more than one of these women to lean on is even better. I have multiple at all times.

You will also be accountable to your higher power, which we will refer to as God. Being honest in prayer, meditation, mindfulness, or any other form of quiet worship is essential. You can lie to yourself, you can even lie to others, but there is always the truth of an experience, and that is what we need to learn to value. I'm still working on this, and can tell you, it is critical to a full life. It is also deeply freeing as you come to know there is a space where only truth lives, and that you can access it when you are ready.

The single most important person you will be honest with and accountable to is you. Through this process, you will become someone you can count on for support and love. If you take each value into your life, nurture it, and practice it fearlessly, before long, it will become second nature. The other distractions will fall away, and you will be left standing with a woman you can be proud of and rely on. This starts with being honest with yourself first and always. It won't be perfect, even decades down the road, but you will get more consistent. For now, just know that is an end goal. As you are fully accountable to and honest with yourself, the rest will fall into place, and integrity will be the natural fruit of your hard work.

One last concept I want to discuss is accountability as a gift. When others know you will own up to your part, they feel less defensive. This is a gift to them. When you know you have the courage to own your part and feel that trust start to come in from others, it is a gift to you. Even God is given the gift of not having to remind you of how rarely you are truly a victim, and how often you have much more power than you realize. You need to exercise and strengthen those courage muscles. It's okay to start with small steps in accountability by acknowledging your voice was more aggressive than the situation needed, or that you did, in fact, get distracted with the computer and forget to start dinner. What are a few little things, or one area of your life you can be more honest in? Try it out and record in your recovery journal how it feels. Was it empowering? Scary? Calming? Triggering? Did you have any insights into why you are dishonest? If you own it with yourself, your higher power, and the people most affected, you are not only accountable, but *fully* accountable. Go you! We will touch more on accountability in many of the other value chapters. It is a foundational skill in recovery. Work to understand and integrate it into your life.

1. In what areas of life have I been less than fully accountable?
2. In what ways can I be more accountable to myself?
3. Are there things I need to be accountable to God for?
4. Who are the three to five women I can count on to hold me accountable with love and courage?
5. What one, small commitment can I make right now to start on my path of being accountable in recovery? (i.e. no more excuses for being late; own my part in a missed deadline; do not embellish or exaggerate when I tell a story.)

6. What worries/scares me most about being fully accountable?

7. Am I afraid I cannot be loved if I make mistakes? Where might this have come from, and what can I do to take my power back now?

Remember, no one is perfect. If you are trying to be, you are not going to be able to do what is necessary to change the path of your life.

Investigation

A deep look at our behaviors, beliefs, and triggers gives us vital information for a solid recovery foundation.

Investigation can be easily summed up in the concept of compassionate curiosity. It is entirely possible you have never asked yourself many of the questions I am going to have you think about throughout this chapter. As you grow in recovery, you will get more rigorous. For example, what I now consider a relapse in myself would not have even made my awareness years ago. My awareness has branched to other areas of my life. I love this, because as we dig deep into our compulsive behaviors and the beliefs that drive them, we become open to other areas that need improvement. Recovery can then go deep in each area, and wide as it spreads through our lives. A few areas of intimacy (a.k.a. relationship with others) to consider inventorying: spiritual, romantic, social, sexual, physical, mental, financial, intellectual, emotional and professional. You may find other areas you find important. Awesome! Count those, too! This is your journey, and you know what areas need the most attention right now. Select three to five, no more, as you go through the process this time. You can add more later. I am not going to dig deep into every type of intimacy in this book, as that is an entirely separate program. I will touch on a few of the most important areas of healthy intimacy for early recovery. For the others, trust your instinct on what these words mean right now. As I have, you will probably adjust as you get stronger and deeper into your healing journey. For now, determine just a few types of intimacy as you read through these sections, and only work those questions in your recovery journal.

Spiritual

This form of intimacy is about your relationship with God and your own Spirit. We are not just complex cells roaming around with no purpose. We have a divine Creator, and He wants to connect with us. He can also help us connect to ourselves and others in spiritual ways. Anytime you feel a soul-to-soul connection, you are connecting through your spirit. A soul *is* the body and spirit. One deeply destructive spiritual habit is judging the soul of another as "shame-based" or deciding we know what someone else is thinking, feeling, or should do. For example, we all go into shame. You can tell when you are in shame, because you might feel small, weak, helpless, or on the other hand, you might feel superior to others, or like if they just did things your way, everything would be fine. It may be true that you know a better way, but it's not okay to insist others "obey" you, do what you say, or to give them unsolicited advice. An adult with healthy boundaries will not tell another adult what they "should" do unless they are asked for ideas. Likewise, an adult living a recovered life will not decide when another person is "in shame," and they certainly won't diagnose it out loud. These are judgment calls outside of the necessary judgment of who is safe and who is not. In fact, either of these behaviors make the one "advising" or diagnosing an unsafe spiritual and emotional source of support. This is because even God does not give unsolicited advice or judge without all the information. Since only He has all the information, He is also the only one qualified to ever diagnose the emotions of another person definitively. Even then, however, I don't think I've ever read a story of Him doing that in scripture, so maybe we should also refrain. Such advice giving and judgment is in direct opposition to the Love of God, which values and cherishes every individual. Additionally, God does not tell others "You are a sinner" He encourages them to get curious about themselves by stating principles of truth and examples of what is right. *That* is how to be spiritually intimate with another Soul.

There is still so much more to this, but what you have now will get you started on the right path. I'll give you just a few questions to ask yourself about how you are doing with spiritual intimacy to help you conceptualize a little better. When you need to assess a situation, do you do so compassionately, even if you need to set boundaries? When someone shares an intimate part of their lives, do you hold it in reverence and care, or do you judge and label them, trying to solve their problem instead of supporting them? Are you uncomfortable in spiritual settings that may not be your own? If nothing illegal or harmful is happening, chances are judgment is in play. As we learn to be compassionate and gentle with ourselves and others, our entire psyche relaxes. We don't have to agree with or fully understand each other, but if our spirits are well inventoried and managed, we can still see the good intentions, even if we disagree on the application.

Romantic

Romantic intimacy is the flirting, fun, tantalizing intimacy shared between two people. When a married woman is spending this highly charged energy on a man (or woman!) other than her spouse, she is on dangerous ground. Furthermore, this is the beginning of an emotional affair. How are your relationships with the others in your life? I get that flirting and getting that attention back is exciting. The playful banter has no place outside of marriage if we want to protect our hearts and keep our heads where they belong. I used to flirt like I was breathing, without realizing it. That doesn't mean I was innocent, it means I was numb and irresponsible with my sexual and romantic power. Flirting is a big part of singlehood, and hopefully marriage. Do we use it wisely and take seriously the emotions and desires it incites? You are not responsible for what another person does with your behavior, but you are certainly responsible for the intentional misuse of your sexuality. Don't play with the fire of romantic attraction and language.

Social

Social intimacy represents our relationships with friends and others we encounter out in the world. How do we treat others? Are we kind? Do we show respect and kindness to everyone? Is there any group of people we feel are less than us, or at least less deserving of respect? Do we shout loudly and forcefully that *our* voice must be heard, then refuse to listen to someone else's voice? How we treat others says so much more about us than it does about them. Sadly, many of our behaviors are learned. Thankfully, we can choose to release them and do things differently!

Sexual

Sexual intimacy is what most people think of when we do talk about intimacy, and it is more than the act of sex. It is about how we interact with every person we come into contact with, and how we choose to characterize ourselves with others. How do we portray ourselves as women? I find this definition valuable and have often been chagrined to realize I have been irresponsible with my sexual interactions. Looking back is a little sobering, especially in this arena of intimacy. This definition further encourages us to see ourselves as whole individuals. Being a woman is not being a second-class citizen. Women carry life within them, bringing it into the world as another being. We breathe life into a house, creating a home and family for our loved ones. We cry with others in pain, and naturally reach out to comfort, creating safety and space for their pain. This sexual power to create is God-given. Respect for and careful use of this gift is the greatest power we can wield as women. Let's be responsible with it.

One of my most favorite quotes was given in a small meeting in Houston, Texas a few years ago. Rhyll Crowshaw, Founder of SA Lifeline and an amazing woman, was asked why she advocates for women in recovery. "When women recover, societies recover." I love this and find it to be so true. We have much more impact than we give ourselves credit for. How are you using your power as a woman? Are you recovering love and happiness, or breaking yourself and others down? Are you flirting to feel good about yourself, or dressing to make other women feel inferior or less attractive? Just take a look and consider how you can be more compassionate and responsible with your sexuality. I'm not saying dress like a hobo, just to be aware of your motives for what you do and why. That energy goes with you and is destructive when used to cut others down or toy with their emotions. You don't want that karmic beating up of others coming back on you. Trust me, it is not worth it!

Physical

Physical intimacy is any touching, kissing, hugging, or other physical contact with another human being. Who do we let into our bubbles of personal space? Do we want them there? Is it appropriate? Am I comfortable with this level of physical intimacy with this person? Would my husband be okay with this level of physical intimacy I'm engaging in with others? We get to decide who gets into our personal bubbles, what they can and cannot do within that bubble, and how long they can stay there. We have just as much responsibility to monitor who comes into our physical space as we do to keep out those whom we want to keep out. We must also be responsible with how we enter the physical space of others.

Professional

Now for professional intimacy. When we work with the same people day after day, relationships naturally form. There is nothing wrong with that. Those relationships need to be appropriate, however. Excessive (some say any) time alone with others we may develop feelings for, or that may undermine committed relationships, need special care. Because I am attracted to men, I watch my relationships with men more closely. Some women reading this may also, or only, be attracted to women. That, then, is where the boundaries go. I've learned a good rule of thumb is, "If my spouse, boss, or a friend who knows my challenges fully were to see this, would they take issue?" If the answer is "Yes," *get out*! Don't play with your heart or anyone else's! Again, not cool to mess with people's minds, including your own. Be nice!

Emotional

Emotional intimacy is a measurement of how close we feel to an individual. It addresses the level of detail-sharing and emotional topics we discuss. Deep emotional sharing can be cathartic in the right setting. It allows us to be vulnerable and ask for help. Emotional intimacy is critical to long-term intimate relationships. The emotional health of a relationship will indicate its overall health more than any other form of intimacy. Here is where honesty, humility and deeper commitment are bred and nurtured. When we are able to be emotionally intimate with those closest to us, healing takes place. Emotional intimacy is the most delicious and nurturing form of intimacy we can share with multiple people. It is also the most alluring, destructive, and potentially dangerous form of intimacy. When we are not getting it in our closest relationships, it becomes very easy to get out of balance in other relationships. Without meaning to, we start to create what I call chaotic intimacy. We see the emotional intensity as connection and love. We see the chaos as intimacy, when it is actually manipulation of our emotions or someone else's. Manipulating another person's emotions in this way is destructive to the relationship, and quite honestly, it is mean. Our hunger for closeness drives us to irrational behaviors while dissolving boundaries. In the example I'll share below, look for how emotional intimacy went too far and made questionable behavior dangerous.

Intellectual

Intellectual intimacy is one that has been most tricky for one particular client of mine. She's what I like to call a "high input/high output" individual. This means she needs a great deal of intellectual stimulation, coupled with outlets to express herself. It took her a while to realize she used this as an excuse to have long, isolated conversations with colleagues – male and female. "We're just chatting," she'd tell herself (and anyone who questioned her, including me). And yet it laid the groundwork for deeper feelings and a breakdown of emotional boundaries. Flirting became okay, and she started to look forward to these conversations with one "friend at work" in particular. Before long, she lost focus and was in over her head. This guy was single, but she was not. What started out as friendly conversation was treading on dangerous ground. Emotional, romantic, professional, and intellectual boundaries had been crossed. When pressed, so were sexual boundaries, though "only" in her head. It did not matter his intents or what boundaries he did or did not cross, it only mattered what was in her heart and mind.

Boundaries

More than once I have talked to women who want to live a recovered life, and who don't know how to set any boundaries. It is stressful in the beginning, but it does get easier. I touch on boundaries a few times in this book, but not nearly enough. It is critical you learn to do this. The longer we let others cross our physical boundaries, the longer it takes to learn to set emotional, sexual, and other boundaries. As physical boundaries are easier to define, they are a great place to start. The importance of physical boundaries cannot be overstated in recovery. Learn them, set them, reinforce them. If someone does not honor your boundaries, you have every right to keep distance between you. And remember, boundaries are about you. What will *you* do in a situation that feels threatening? We cannot, and should not try, to control another person. We can walk away or make protective decisions when others prove to be unsafe.

Ladies, our heads need to stay where they belong, and there is no space at work, play, church, school, volunteer projects, or anywhere else for letting down our boundaries. I share the story above to illustrate the need to always keep our hearts protected, and to always keep boundaries in place. If there is an intimacy level for it, there needs to be a boundary. If we call it a boundary, that is because intimacy is possible. This story also shows how the crossing of one type of boundary facilitates the breakdown of other boundaries.

You might be feeling a little overwhelmed with all of this. It is a lot to keep track of, and a great deal more to work through. You cannot and should not try to work through it all at once. Yes, it is important to grow in responsibility, honesty, all of the awesome values covered in this book, and you cannot possibly tackle it all at once. So, right now I want you to take a break. Write down what you are feeling, have a cup of lemonade or hot cocoa, do a little self-care and let your mind relax. You can come back for more later. Whatever you do, clear your mind and relax for at least fifteen minutes. But maybe avoid social media so you don't get into distraction!

◊◊◊

I truly hope you took my advice! How did it feel to take care of yourself? I hope you enjoyed it. This is a skill you'll need for the rest of your life. While we are on the topic, how is your day-to-day and month-to-month self-care? Are you taking breaks like you need? Are you filling your own emotional tank so you can love better? Girl, you matter! Take care of you, or it will bite you in the backside! Maybe it's a good time to take another break and inventory how you are taking care of yourself in all of these areas. Are you giving yourself healthy outlets? If you need some ideas, I'll keep a running list up on HerRecoveryRoadmap.com for you. Feel free to visit and steal some ideas!

Ready to talk more about this investigation topic? I'm sure you realize how much there is to look at. Don't overwhelm yourself. Take it a concept at a time and report it to your accountability partner or a friend in recovery. If you are part of a group, find women there to connect and check in with. If not, find a group. You need other women!

My suggestion here is to write down or print out these questions (I have a PDF on the website). Think about them, take time with them, and come back to them as you need to. Even in a consistently recovered life, it is an excellent idea to revisit these questions every few months. At the very least, you'll want to take inventory annually to keep tabs on yourself in areas you may be slipping. Recovery is, after all, a continual process that gets more and more rigorous as we go along. And without investigation, managing recovery is impossible because you will have no idea what you are managing. Here are a few questions to start with:

- What behaviors do I engage in that attempt to illicit feelings or a reaction from another person in some way? (emotional, sexual, romantic, or otherwise).
- What do I do that makes others feel uncomfortable?
- Who and what do I blame for how I behave?
- What thoughts and beliefs drive my actions?
- Am I honest in all that I do and say?
- Do I think it is okay to keep back part of the truth?
- Do I spend money I don't have on things I don't need?
- Do I meet all financial obligations every month? (I ask about money because most women have a little thing I call the Addictive Triad. Most, maybe all of us, act out in sex, money, and food in some way. It can be helpful to stay aware of all three components of the AT. I don't know where this concept originally came from, but I've used it with much success since a client brought it to my attention.)
- Do I make excuses for poor or irresponsible behavior?
- Do I try to cover up my mistakes, or let others take the fall for them?
- Do I expect others to make me feel better?
- Do I use my emotions to hold others hostage?
- Do I pretend to be more hurt or angry than I am?
- Do I pretend I'm fine when I'm actually hurt or angry?
- Do I seek attention in situations where it is inappropriate?

- Do I break the law, even in small ways, then justify it?
- Are there things about me I fear others would judge or reject me for?
- How do I respond when things don't go how I think they should?
- Am I flexible, or do I become upset when plans change?
- Do I feel victimized by others, or powerless to create the life I want?
- What are the excuses I make for not having the life I say I want?
- How did I end up where I am? What was my part?
- How have I used my losses, abuses, or traumas to justify my behaviors?
- Do I feel others owe me?
- Do I often feel better than or less than others? If so, when and how? (You can feel both, even in the same situation.)
- Do I need external validation to feel valued, loved, or worthy?
- Do I overeat or not eat enough?
- Do I oversleep or not sleep enough?
- Do I over-exercise or not exercise enough?
- Do I overspend, or refuse to spend money to take care of myself?
- Do I make commitments I have no intention of keeping?
- Do I make commitments, then not follow through?

- Do I compare my life, my marriage, my home, or my family to other people?
- When I compare do I come up lacking or superior?
- Do I neglect to take care of myself, then become upset at others for their expectations of me?
- How do I respond when others do not meet my expectations?
- Do I communicate my expectations clearly and respectfully?
- Do I feel entitled to give other adults, or children that are not mine, unsolicited advice?
- Do I feel that if people would just listen to me, their lives would be better?
- Do I say things like "I told you so" or "If only you had…"?
- Do I ask for explanations when something was clearly an accident?

There are many more questions we can ask ourselves. In fact, the list could easily be a book by itself. The key is to start investigating what we are doing and why in our relationships. Then we can start learning to manage what is not working. It is also likely we will see more behaviors we'd like to change as we go along. This is normal, and a good thing. Take mental note or record it on a running list and keep working on what you are already doing. The other things will come back up as you are ready. You do not need to tackle it all at once or overwhelm yourself with an intense 100-page list. Maybe take a few questions at a time, or even just one, and really dig into it.

As you do, you will find you end up answering others naturally as you just keep writing. I like to take one or two questions from a list like this, and work on them for my daily recovery journaling. The next day, I'll pick one or two more. It's great.

As we get better and better at living a recovered life, it becomes easier to spot the lies we tell and the unhealthy, compulsive patterns we have not noticed before. It helps to always be looking for places to be more accountable or honest with ourselves. This is where ongoing inventory is helpful. You took years to become the person you are now. While it won't take as long to learn new behaviors, it will take at least some time. Be patient with yourself and stay curious about places to improve. Needing work and being aware of that work is a sign of a woman of integrity. Go get it, woman!

Triggers

Let's talk about triggers and how to manage them. You need to know what brings up emotion in you, then you need to know what does and does not work for managing those emotions. For example, I know women who make phone calls to individuals that support them in recovery, and some who support them in damaging behaviors. Some women binge eat, some starve; some run a mile or two, some watch an entire season of whatever is available. It is our job to manage how we take the triggers and what we do with them afterward. The triggers I mean here are any emotions, no matter if you see them as good or bad, that may leave you feeling discomfort. If you feel an emotion, then reach for your phone, it's probably a good time to investigate what's up in your head. Now and then, just unwinding to a good show is helpful. It can also be a way to shut emotions off. Only you can know what is really helpful and what is your way of hiding or distracting yourself. An insightful question from a friend can help you stay in truth. The temptation is to justify what numbs us. Numb can be such a relief! And hours later, we come out of the binge coma and nothing has changed, *plus* now the kids are hungry, or the deadline is closer. I want to help you stop doing this to yourself, and the only way is through honest inventory of how you shut down, when, and for how long. After an honest look there, you'll need to develop an accountability plan. As I've helped various women take these steps, it is awesome to watch them light up with hope and courage. Maintaining that requires continued support, so make sure you get that in place if you don't have it already.

Emotions are tricky. They almost seem to sneak up on us. If we are not careful they can take over our lives, sabotaging the life of integrity we are trying to live. Learning to handle emotions in helpful ways makes those emotions less of a threat. I like to go for a run, then talk issues out with a friend. Journaling and self-reflection to understand my part and what I can do now to move toward the results I want are also useful. Early in recovery I came across a series of questions that I've since seen in one form or another multiple times. Here I share them with you in the language I have found most helpful. I have no idea where this concept originally came from, so if you find out, let me know!

1. What just happened that did not go well?
2. How do I wish things had gone better?
3. What did go well that I can build on?
4. What will I do differently next time?
5. How can I better prepare for future situations that might be similar?

These questions can be a quick way to bring yourself into honest reflection. After all, we are the only ones who can make the changes needed for new dynamics in our relationships. These reflections help manage that responsibility.

Also evaluating why we become upset about something moves us toward a more recovered life. For example, we only get stage fright because we care about the outcome of going on stage. We also only get upset about an event when we care about what is happening. Being upset means whatever you are doing, about to do, being told, or thinking about, matters to you. Great! Now what will you do about it? What is it that matters so much? What were you hoping would happen that didn't? Is that a fair expectation, and is it your place to hold that expectation in this situation or for this person? Is this in your power, and if so, what can you do to make things better for everyone involved while being honest and responsible? Again, the inquiry can go on and on. Don't get over whelmed, just learn to ask yourself the right questions. In the groups I host, we get to experience doing this by asking each other deep and poignant questions. I strongly suggest locating significant others who can help you dig deeper in honesty. No one ever got fully into honesty on their own. We all need help sometimes, and that's not a bad thing. It keeps us from getting stuck and stagnating. It is also critical to get out of your own thought patterns and beliefs by talking them through with someone else.

As usually happens, historical events and old feelings creep in. Investigate why these still hold power, and what you can do to neutralize them. The present is the only place you can change anything. That won't stop the past from being influential in the now … until you learn to manage it. As I've said, management can only come after honest investigation. So, dig in as those things come up! Hire a therapist for serious trauma or abuse. Spending too much time in the past will keep you stuck, as it did me for a long time. But reframing those experiences as potential learning experiences and places to draw courage and strength from *will* help you recover. You made it this far, my friend, you clearly have grit and personal strength. Now dig deep and let it help you forgive, make restitution when you need to, and most importantly, let it teach you compassion and love for yourself. You've made it through some hard crap to get this far. Now, build on what you have overcome while you look to the future. One concept at a time, do better each day. It gets easier, I promise!

Chapter
5

Empowerment through Courage

We must learn to courageously empower ourselves and those around us to live a life of honesty and integrity, without excuse or justification.

Courage might not be the first thing you considered needing when starting this journey, but let me tell you, it is critical. I love so many of the other ways to say courage: guts, grit, empowerment, fearlessness, valor, heroism, bravery, so many more. Right now, I am talking about all of those. And I want to tell you, I know you have what this takes inside of you, because you are still here. You haven't given up. You've got this, my friend.

Choosing to live a life of integrity is not the easy path. The world won't notice, much less appreciate it. This is not about the world, it is about you. It takes insane amounts of guts to stand up in a group of women, crooning over an attractive man, and walk away. You might lose friends as you move away from the socially acceptable habit of fantasy and distraction through lust. Heaven forbid you should tell women who laugh about these things and take the visions of other men into their bedrooms that they are lusting! However, your courage will inspire other women and you will be doing them a loving service. It will invite them to wake up to the reality of their thoughts, words, and eventual actions. As you move more and more into a life full of integrity, it will become natural to share what you have learned. Just remember, most of the time it's not appropriate to just tell someone else, especially an adult, what to do. It is always okay to stand up for your own values though! You do that by openly addressing, or not participating in what is happening in these conversations. I find it easiest to ask curious questions like these:

- My husband would feel hurt if he knew I talked about another man like that. Can we please change the conversation?
- I'm not comfortable talking about him (the "hot" local doctor). Can we change the subject?
- I understand not everyone feels this way, but I really don't enjoy movies that get adult women all hot and bothered by teenage boys. I want to go to a movie, but can we go to something else? (Then be willing to not attend if consensus is the sexy drama or romantic comedy)

Do you see why this takes courage? You are empowering yourself to hold boundaries, to maintain your values, and to live in integrity. That's huge! At the same time, you are allowing other women to perhaps see something they have not before. That something just might save hurt feelings, or ever her marriage. The kinds of women you are going to want to spend time with in a few months will be open to these changes. And though I know how hard it is to lose popularity at church and in the neighborhood for standing up for something important, I promise it is worth it in the long run. You, those women, and the men they are objectifying, deserve more. Let's be brave.

A woman I love dearly once stood up to what was very possibly headed for an extramarital affair. She tells of how upset she was to have been put in a situation to watch someone she loves flirt with a single man who worked at a café where the two often had lunch. The server often came to chat, giving the women a good amount of extra attention. One day, he sat down with them and put his arm around my friend's lunch companion. Both women had wedding rings on, both had talked about their families. Now, this man was sitting at their table, as if he had any right or reason to be there. Even more, he was now crossing a physical boundary, and she could smell the alcohol on his breath. With all of the love she had in her for the other woman, and all of the righteous anger she could muster, she sent that server packing and turned to her friend. Love was expressed, and new boundaries were set. "I will not watch you mock your marriage. We choose a new place to eat, and you never do anything like this again, or we do not go out together anymore." Talk about guts! I know both women, and will tell you, few relationships have the level of trust and love they now have with each other. Courage. Empowerment. Truth. Love it!

This brave woman set a healthy, appropriate boundary with her friend. No negotiation and no force, just a simple and clear statement that these are the options, and what you just did will never be okay with me. The boundary had one very important component that you need to understand. Did you notice the friend didn't say "You can't do that! I won't let you!" No. She was very clear in a loving way that did not decide for or dictate to the other woman. In effect, she invited her friend into integrity, while stating what she (the first woman) would see as acceptable. For a moment, she was afraid the friendship might be over. Not everyone would put up with being called out like that. And not everyone has the integrity to set a boundary of this caliber with someone they love. It was done to keep them both safe and in a healthy relationship. The motive was love. The line was drawn, but in a way that gave options to the other adult in the situation. As equals, one had no right to demand anything of the other. Their mutual love made this work well for them both.

As friends, they each have a right to be honest, and courageously state what they will and will not be involved in. These boundaries are much scarier than the kind most of us are used to. Growing up, it is common for a child to hear, "Do this, or else." We may even hear things like that from superiors at work who lack proper training. For you and I, who want better, there is more to it than stating a demand. Other adults have agency. While it is fully acceptable to refuse to be part of certain conversations, going to explicit or romantic movies, or reading the latest romance novel in a book club, it is not okay to dictate to other adults what they should or should not do. Kindly, compassionately, and honestly communicating your rules for yourself is part of learning to live a life of integrity. It takes practice, but it gets easier the clearer you get with what is and is not okay with you, for you. Let me give an example of this that includes multiple chances to be courageous while empowering someone you love. This will also help you see what it will look like when someone who loves you is trying to build you up to face a challenge. Notice the lack of problem solving. No problem solving for another adult! It's degrading, not to mention rude if they don't want advice. Got it? Excellent.

Let's say you know your sister has been using pornography alone at night and she is now expressing disinterest in being sexually intimate with her husband. She is upset that he is upset. It is loving to first ask if you can share what you see. She says no, you let it go. That's it! She says yes, you have a green light. Let her know you see and love her first, then give her the insights you have. "I get how messy sex can be in marriage, with you both working and having two kids on top of it. I remember that stress. You sound really lost, and I want to help if I can. I know you've been staying up watching pornography. Since it has been found to decrease sex drive and attraction toward live partners in men, especially in marriage, do you see how it is probably impacting you as well? While men and women have some differences, I can't imagine this isn't affecting you." She tells you no way, it's because her husband is lazy, won't help with the kids, and is always wanting sex. Wow, that's a lot of information, right? It feels tempting to jump in and point out how she has been complaining about the same thing for five years and refuses to talk to him about marriage counseling or setting any boundaries for helping out since they both work full time. Just trust me, this will not help. In fact, she isn't looking to get to the bottom of things, maybe isn't even ready to take responsibility. That's another conversation. For this one, think about what you would do. What would you say? Take a minute to process that.

Historically, I'd want to keep trying to get her to see she is not helping herself. Now I see the game, even though she isn't playing it intentionally. She needs to be heard, seen, and is probably overwhelmed. No one can fix anything well in that mindset. She needs to be encouraged to resolve the excuses, and deal with the real problem at hand. This has nothing to do with dishes, diapers, or working late. It is all about a lack of nurturing, honest, responsible communication between committed partners. The truth is, however, she's not going to make any movement, no matter what, until she is ready to see her part. Give her a little more love and get off the phone before you just *have to* give her advice. She's an adult, and when she is ready, she will ask you for feedback. If she isn't asking, she isn't ready or she doesn't want advice from you. Breathe and do the grown-up thing: bite your tongue unless she asks.

Lust

The Bible says to look upon a woman to lust after her is to commit sin. Why do women think we get off the hook? I assure you, we don't. If objectifying women through pornography is something you are not okay with your husband doing, how do you feel about him thinking "Well, hello!" when a beautiful, seductively-dressed woman walks by? I know I'd be in hubby's face so fast he'd need to know what day it was. So why do we engage in these thoughts and conversations and "like" them on social media? Why do women get a free pass to do the very things we get so hurt and angry at men over?

Now do you see why courage is included? I'm not kidding when I say you might lose friends when you take a stand against female lust and fantasy. I certainly did. And more friends who resonate with the type of life you want to live will find their way to you. They are worth the wait and a few girl's night movies out alone if necessary.

It also takes courage to accept feedback from others. Remember my friend's lunch companion? She is a brave soul. She did not become defensive or angry. She saw the truth, apologized, and chose the friendship over her own lust and pride. They never did go back to that café. Being called out, even by someone who loves you, can hurt. The pain may even have shame attached to it, as it does for many people. Learning to hear the meaning and love behind the words is a skill. It takes self-talk and time to sift through our interpretation of what was said, and what was really meant. Then you have to be honest about feelings that come up. It's incredibly risky to be willing to take that kind of correction! No wonder so many women don't. It is uncomfortable to hear when behaviors are offensive to others. It is scary, and it usually stinks. Being told a certain thought or behavior is lustful and objectifying feels horrible. However, if you want to truly live the kind of life you say you do, you'll need to learn to take this kind of feedback. This will also come in useful when you need to apologize and the person is in a good place to talk openly. If you empower them to be honest, most people will tell you what upsets them. That means you'll be hearing how others feel about something you did or said. Only a woman who knows she has value beyond her mistakes can take this kind of feedback. It's uncomfortable, and so very good for you! It helps to have another friend or family member to go to for a hug and reassurance that you are still a good person and can take steps to fix just about anything. I often need this after inviting honest conversation about myself. It further empowers all involved, and sometimes asking for the hug takes its own level of courage when we've misbehaved.

This brings me to another type of courage. Living in fantasy and emotional distraction hurts those around us. You may find many people you need to repair relationships with. There are always others to attempt to make amends to. Sincere apology, with no excuses or justification, is the best start. No matter what anyone else did, you are responsible for what *you* did. That's not to say abuse is ever the victim's fault. It certainly never is. Abuse, neglect, or a spouse's affair or indiscretions, do not justify yours. Those things matter, and your actions after do not make someone else's matter less. Your sincere apology, without excusing it because they did something first, opens the door for them. It gives another person the opportunity to walk, with courage, into an honest interaction with you. They may choose to take responsibility for their part, and that's great. Thank them. Then move on to how you can make amends to them for any hurt or loss they suffered. For example, if you stole money, repay it, and then some. If you caused legal harm, do you need to report yourself?

A word of caution, this never means a target or his intimate partner! That's a great way to cause more harm and put yourself in jeopardy of things getting out of hand, fast. More importantly, you may cause harm to a marriage you have no business involving yourself in. If that sounds harsh, I'm sorry. When you have space from him, and gain some ground in living with integrity, you'll be glad you kept your mouth shut on this one. If you're not, then the relationship in your head needs another dose of reality and another round of repentance/ clearing out. Don't think I don't know how much you want to make things right. I promise you, I know. It is really hard to just stay away. You've done enough. Find another way to make amends. In fact, this book is part of my journey with this very thing. Think on it, pray about it, meditate on it, but do not go near that woman. She does not need that hurt or worry in her life. This is between her and her husband now. Stay out of it!

Ultimately, our consequences are not up to us. Only living in integrity and with courage are. Facing consequences can be one of the scariest parts of recovery. Don't give up though. Take time with it and be wise. Seek legal counsel first, if needed. Most of us don't face any legal repercussions, but that doesn't necessarily make it easier to take responsibility for past mistakes. Have the courage to do it anyway, then forgive yourself. Moving on is not for the faint of heart, either. You've already started the journey. Hang in there.

"Love"

Now for a potentially painful bucket of ice water. Let's talk about the courage to face what is and is not "love." My friend, if you keep telling yourself you love him, and "him" is not your hubby, the relationships is based on lies, distortion of reality, and a whole lot of denial. I care too much about you to let you keep thinking you love this other man, real or fantasy. If he is a real person who tells you he loves you, you need to get the hot mess out of there, fast. That is probably very hard to hear, and you might be justifying why your relationship is different than other women's right now. Stop. Just stop and hear me out. I don't need to know his motives for that crap, and neither do you; you are a married woman! Even if you are a separated or a filing-for-divorce woman, you are not free. If he is married, even more crazy-making is going on. And a relationship that began with either of you married to someone else is not going to be in anyone's best interest. It is tantalizing, it feels sexy, and you feel 100 percent certain you have found your soul mate. What you have found is a karmic relationship. This relationship was created by the universe, with your unconscious collaboration, to show you where you are not being honest with yourself. It is based on intensity, fantasy, and is covering up some hard facts about your marriage, your past, or your relationship with yourself. Start digging. What is it covering up? What is the real pain, anger, or unresolved trauma swimming around convincing you this new guy will make you happier? There are all sorts of reasons you cannot keep that relationship going. Be brave. Be strong. Be courageous. Empower yourself and empower him to *move on*! Let this guy go. Cry, hurt, feel the loss, and know we will be talking about sacrifice before this book is over. It hurts, I know. You still need to move on, completely. Don't run from the truth, or you will never stop doing this to yourself.

Anything that pulls you away from a committed relationship romantically, sexually, or intellectually, even a rocky committed relationship, is an affair. You are not the kind of woman who truly wants to have an affair. I know this because you are reading my book, and it was written for women like us. We are women who hide, running away from vulnerability and discomfort like frightened kittens, but we don't truly want to hurt anyone. We lash out, we make up a safe reality, and we hurt, deeply. These fantasies feel more real than our husbands and children because we have gotten so good at using them to mask anything we feel too hopeless or afraid to tackle. Again, you are reading this book, and have not tossed it yet. That means you know it is for you, and you want to do things differently. The first step to becoming the woman you are meant to be, is to admit to yourself you need to make major changes in how and with whom you interact on a regular basis. Things will get back to normal soon. Right now, you have asked for my help. Trust me then. He is not what you really need, he won't make you happy, and you are worth more than a second-rate relationship, fantasy or otherwise. You are worth more. It's time you sent that message to the universe, then picked up on it for yourself. You deserve better. Create it.

In closing on this topic, living the values taught in this book will make you a beacon to other women who are hungry for more than the status quo. Your change in attitude, beliefs about yourself and others, and the way you carry yourself, will empower those around you. They will seek what you have, and you will have the chance to share, leading others to newfound contentment. Being looked up to is a big responsibility, which requires staying humble. Always remember what it felt like to be hopeless and alone. Be kind to these women, remembering to keep your own boundaries about what you will and will not condone. Protect your own need for reflective time and sanity. Do all of this with the gentle strength only a woman of integrity can claim. It will help you love those who are difficult to love, forgive those you thought you could never forgive, and most importantly, you will come to see the courage you had all along. Walk in it. Let it go before you to light the darkness. Before long, you might even find yourself ready to truly lead and guide other women. Embrace this by seeking others, further along, to help you do so responsibly. Do not hide from the strong, courageous, beautiful woman you have always had inside you, and who is now blossoming for the world to witness.

Chapter
6

Honesty

A woman who is not honest in all her interactions, cannot maintain a recovered life for long. Integrity and peace of mind will elude her.

I have worked with numerous women over the years who don't feel they can tell their intimate partners, parents, or others the truth. At the end of the discussion, it all comes down to the same thing, no matter how they word it: they are afraid. Some of the fears are about hurting others more than they have, and I get that. But the deeper we dig together, the more I realize it comes down to one main fear. "What if he can't love me anymore once he knows everything?" The fear is real. Many divorces happen over indiscretions like those we are talking about. And many relationships survive, even thrive, after complete honesty has opened the door to trust.

I understand the worry. By the time they reach this level of honesty, women are usually dedicated to doing their part to save the relationships that mean the most. This is most likely the place you are at, and it is the best place to be. You need real answers, not imaginary answers based in fear of the unknown. These fears are shadows, not reality, and you are ready for more responsible information.

Honesty is a concept we are all familiar with. Most children are taught to tell the truth from a young age. It's a given for instructing children in societies and cultures around the world. Yet somehow, we all also learn it is okay to tell white lies or leave out little parts of the truth to protect others. "I don't want to hurt them more than I have," or "He wouldn't understand, so it is better this way." These are very real emotions, and we've all felt them in some form or another. Since we are talking about honesty though, I need you to brace yourself for a painful truth. In reality, we leave out part of the truth to protect ourselves from the consequences of another seeing us fully. The worry is real, he might be more hurt. He might end the relationship. And I love you too much to not tell you the truth as I have seen it in every relationship: that is his choice to make, not yours. No matter your history, no matter what happened to you that dug you deeper into the decisions you made, they are still decisions *you* made. *This* decision is not yours. I do highly recommend full disclosure with a well-trained therapist. Details are not necessary, but there is a fine line between not causing unnecessary pain and keeping secrets.

Even as I write this, I see how there are additional boundaries I can put in place that will keep me in a good place. They may look like removing, even blocking certain email addresses or phone numbers. Clean up social media or quit it all together if needed. It's also okay to sleep on the couch for a few nights to give you both space. These boundaries are for me, and he deserves to not need to worry or be reminded of my compulsive, irresponsible decisions. So, I will put those in place without looking back. He doesn't need to ask me to do this or approve them as necessary. They are my responsibility, not his. It is my responsibility to ask him to communicate how he is feeling, so I can honor that. The beautiful part is, we have grown so much closer through all of this. After all, we both had ugly things to ask forgiveness for, and that has also helped. Even if he wasn't sorry though, I would be, for my part. You don't need to have done something serious to have a reason to apologize and set new boundaries. And his transgressions are not an excuse to hide your own.

Do you see how your honesty is not determined by what others want from you? They are in pain. They have been hurt. They have been lied to and deceived. That sucks! It sucks for them, and it sucks for you, because you must deal with seeing it. It is worth it though, if you are also willing to be fully responsible, and do what needs to be done. If you're not willing to take that responsibility, you are not truly in recovery, and need to take inventory of why. There are many questions at the end of this chapter to help you do just that. Please use them and do all you can to get to a place where truth overrides your fear.

I do have one caveat to "do what needs to be done" to make up for your choices. Yes, you've made mistakes, and yes, they are a big deal. That does *not* mean you are now eternally indebted to this person! Your emotions, actions, and mistakes are for *you* to learn from. They are painful gifts of awareness and light that will help *you* become the woman you were always meant not be. They are not chains and prison cells of indebtedness. Yes, you need to take responsibility and stop the excuses. No, this is not a life sentence of servitude. Having appropriate boundaries around not acting in – or out – anymore are critical. You also need boundaries around the level of consequence you receive. What I mean by this is, emotional manipulation, telling everyone what you have done, and punishing you are not okay. Sleeping on the coach for a while, him needing a couple of close friends or family members to confide in or wanting to go to therapy are 100 percent appropriate expectations (I actually insist my clients see a marriage therapist if a physical affair has occurred. Not a bad idea otherwise if either of you feel you need it). Remember, the decisions made by you were yours. These are his. He can be hurt, angry, whatever else he wants or needs to be. But he doesn't get to "make you pay" until the end of time. Days, weeks of sorting through his feelings and the needs he will have for building trust is absolutely reasonable. During that time, many more honest conversations (and your validating him) need to happen. When you need support, ask for it. Just make sure your support comes from a responsible woman who understands the depth of his pain and your part in it. That way, she can validate you, love you, reassure you, and give you what you need as your partner figures things out. Then she can send you lovingly back into life.

Your Pain

Now I want to talk for a few minutes about your pain, and the hurts you have suffered. It is entirely possible your dear hubby has inflicted some of that pain. In fact, he probably did. That is *not* a free pass, any more than it means what you have felt isn't important. If you need to talk about tough things, like his indiscretions, his pornography usage, the way he manipulates you into sex or violates your trust through his relationships with other women (including his mother), that is important to discuss. These discussions must not be in the attitude of "he did that first, so I did this." Many women are hurt by their husbands, and they don't do what you did. This is not about excuses, justifications, blame, or finger-pointing. Where one partner has a sex-based compulsion, the other might as well. We already know yours. Do you need to talk about his? If so, talk to your support first, then go to him, remembering you both have a part in the dynamic you are now in. This might be done best with a well-educated mentor, close friend, coach, or therapist. I do not recommend trying to do it alone until you are both in a less traumatized state.

You may also have pain from the past you need to be honest about. In fact, it would be a major surprise if you have no childhood neglect, abuse, or trauma. Junior high is horrible for most of us. Becoming adults is terrifying for many. What is there that might encourage you to justify how you act in or out? What tells you that you deserve the pain or the self-abusing thoughts running through your head? Why do you believe it is alright to behave the ways you have? How have you justified your behaviors in the past? What is something you still justify? If you can pull these beliefs and events from your past and bring them into your current situation, it will help you understand what you do and why. This is a critical step in forgiving yourself. It will also give you a list of hurts you have endured to aid in the healing process. I won't repeat all the clichés you have probably heard hundreds of times, but I do have a valuable piece of advice I learned early in my recovery from anorexia. Forgiveness is not about the other person and whether or not they are sorry. When you can get to a place where it doesn't matter if they apologize, acknowledge the harm they did, or are "doing the right thing," you have done the hard work for yourself. Forgiveness means I don't need them or anything they could ever offer. It is *absolutely* easier to forgive knowing they are sorry. If they can validate, apologize, show how they have changed, it makes forgiving so much easier! This I know and want to validate for you right now. Sure, they "should" be sorry, apologize, and try to help you heal the way you are learning to do for others. It is the right thing to do. You don't *need* it though, because you get to decide how this will impact the rest of your life. My mom sees my pain, she hears it, she tells me how it never should have happened, and how it isn't my fault. She lets me cry, hands me tissues, and hugs me as long as I need afterward. But even before she brought me into her family as her own, I had learned to do this for myself. It is harder, but I want you to understand, you have everything you need to forgive. Having someone hear it and hold space for you and your pain is a gift I hope you can receive. It makes things so much better that much faster, so seek it whenever possible. Not having it, though, will not keep you stuck if you are willing to learn the skills necessary to give this to yourself through your connection with God and the wise woman you have deep inside of you.

With all of this in mind, I have a few journaling prompts and probing questions for you. Take time with this. Connect with your Spiritual Power through whatever means you use and love yourself enough to be totally honest in your responses, perhaps for the first time ever. Don't judge your responses based on what you think I want you to say, or what you think the "right" answer is. I promise, the right answer is the honest, vulnerable, terrifying one deep inside you. Until you see that answer, you'll never know what you need to do from a place of courage. You also don't have to do these in order. Choose an order that makes sense to you, just make sure you take time with each question and prompt.

Think only of your closest one or two relationships. These can be spouse, parents, siblings, close friends, a sponsor or friend in recovery, your support person, even your therapist or religious leader. Feel it out and decide what feels most comforting and healing to you.

1. What hurts in your past do you need to have witnessed by another person? Who is in your life that can hear them?

2. What do you hope they will be able to do for you as they hear your pain? Do you want to have them hold your hand, sit quietly next to you, sit across from you so you can look at them as you need and are ready to? Make a wish list for yourself that you can share with them. Then ask them to do what they are comfortable with. You won't necessarily get all you want, but them knowing what you need and hope for will help you both. It is also a less painful chance to take moments before you share a heartache. If your person is a trusted coach or therapist, know that they cannot offer the physical support you might desire. That's why I encourage you to go to someone who *can* hold your hand, etc. Be realistic in this list, and fully vulnerable, understanding that you can always ask for what you need. Perhaps you won't be ready to share your needs or secrets completely the first time you do this, but it will feel more comfortable as you practice. What do you need to ask for to make this feel okay as you share? Then ask for as much as you can verbally, handing over the list if needed. Let them tell you what they are comfortable with and meet where you are both honored. An "I'm not comfortable holding your hand, but I'll sit by you with my hand on your shoulder or arm" is a very loving compromise. Again, if you are with a professional, you may need to let her handing you the tissue box when the tears start be enough, then get that needed hug from someone else.

3. Now, who in your life can give this to you? Who can you trust to honor your pain and hold it in confidence?

4. Why do you trust these people?

5. Take a moment to call and set up a forty-five- to sixty-minute appointment with one or two of them for as soon as possible to talk through some of that pain. Hurry, before you freak yourself out! Then commit to holding that commitment, no matter what. Obstacles and excuses are already on their way to you. Love yourself enough to do this anyway. Then breathe. If you're not nervous and wanting to back out yet, you will be. Don't let yourself! Keep the meet-ups to no more than sixty minutes at first, so you don't overwhelm yourself or take more time than they may have to give.

6. If you did number five, tell me how you feel in your journal. What is going through your head, and why do you think this will be good? (Even if you doubt how good it is, the fact that you did number five because I told you to *is* proof you see some value in it too.)

7. If you didn't do number five, tell me why in your journal. Address it to me and report out on it. Are you afraid, doubtful, think it's stupid? Tell me! You have my permission to swear and call me names, just get it all out. If you are going to refuse to love

yourself, you deserve to know why, and I want to know, too.

8. Now, let's talk about the other people in your life. Who do you need to come clean with? For the finer details of your emotional, romantic, or intellectual affairs, you only need to come fully clean to your intimate partner and one other person. A religious leader, a parent, your main support person, but you need two people. Who are these two people? You can have more, just keep the number to those closest and who have a need to know. For all other indiscretions, deceptions, harms you have done, lies you have told, the list may be longer. It will also not be as intense. I suggest using as much paper, and as many separate lists as needed. You can group by type of wrong done or by person. Do what works for you; this is a roadmap, not a rigid demand. You do need to do it, though.

9. If the people you are closest to don't know the real, vulnerable, flawed you, do you believe you will be able to trust and love you the way you honestly and truly desire?

10. If they don't know what you have truly done, can they make an informed decision about the relationship like they deserve to be able to make?

11. Do you ever wonder if they would stick around if they did know everything? If so, what questions do you ask yourself about their love for you?

12. Do you believe these questions will ever *truly* go away without you having the courage to be completely honest?

13. What are you afraid will happen if you tell the whole truth? What have you decided they will do that justifies keeping important truths from them?

14. Do you have a right to make this decision for them? If you feel you do, what gives you that power over them and their choices, as adults?

15. What are things you have not been fully honest with each of these people about? Make a separate list for each person.

16. Do you have any desire to be honest and come clean? What does that desire feel like?

17. If you do not have a desire to come clean, why? What does that feel like?

18. If you decide not to be fully honest, you need to make that decision consciously and with all of the information. Know that you will never fully forget and will always carry the deception. It can and will keep you from full recovery, and you will always wonder if the relationship would have survived. I will tell you, they usually do. And for those clients I have had whose intimate partnerships did not make it through full disclosure, they have a peace about the situation those who choose not to disclose never get. Even without the marriage being maintained, it is amazing to see healing come, and these two

people become true friends who can work together for the good of their children. Without complete honesty to re-build the foundation of trust, they know they never would have achieved the kinds of relationships they have. So, I challenge you to start thinking seriously about the level of trust and commitment you want. They go hand-in-hand, so make an intentional decision here. If you will not be fully honest, you are not fully committed to yourself or the one you love. Fear of loss is real for us all. It is no excuse for deception or half-truth.

Chapter

7

The Here and Now

*Now is the time to train our minds to focus on reality, and to
let go of the addictive fantasy life we've been indulging.*

antasy and distraction are usually based in a past
event, future potentiality, or are out of time completely
because they are fictional stories. By focusing on time
out-of-place with where we are, it becomes challenging to
keep track of time's passing. Our whole concept of time can
become warped. This is true of fantasy, and it is true of any
distraction. Social media, the latest Netflix series, planning for
an event, and even responding to email and text messages can
easily steal hours from our days. When this happens, we often
feel increased stress at what still needs to get done. Living
like this is not healthy, and it adds to the need for distraction
from the pain of not feeling like we are getting enough done.

Staying in the present moment is a challenge for most people. It is so easy to let our minds wander. This is especially true for women who struggle with fantasy or any other distraction. There always seems to be something else to look at, think about, or spend emotional energy on. Being serious about living a life of integrity also means learning to live in the present, doing whatever you are doing mindfully. This is a skill that requires practice. You'll also need to put serious effort into it as you begin.

I'm reminded of a friend in recovery who used to use her environment and own voice to keep herself from fantasizing about a friend's husband (or anyone else!) She was at my house one day, and suddenly started talking to herself in the weirdest way. "Salt. That's the salt, it is on the stove. Stove. The salt is next to the pepper on the stove. Pepper. Pepper makes me sneeze and tastes weird. I don't like pepper. I also don't like…" and on she went for about two minutes. I just watched, not quite knowing what was happening. She took a deep breath and turned to me to explain. When she starts to think of him, and can't manage it silently after a few seconds, she forces herself to fill her mind with what is happening in the here and now. She floods it with stimuli she can control. As she explained, I realized she was holding my salt and pepper for most of her process. Physical, emotional, auditory, visual and memory-based stimuli tied her into the moment in her real life, where this man had no place to be. It was impressive. I've used this technique many times since, just to keep myself focused on a lecture, a conversation, or a moment I am wandering from.

Back in about 2010, I kept an AA sobriety chip in my left hand for three days straight. When needed, it was right there. I'd push it firmly into my palm and recite Reinhold Niebuhr's Serenity Prayer. I'd walk, stand in the cold outside, put my hands on the hot concrete, whatever. It didn't matter that AA had nothing to do with what I was focusing on because the chip was the perfect tool for me right then. It simply said, "If nothing changes, nothing changes." These examples are ways to engage the moment as defense against the distractions of our minds. Mindfulness and meditation are excellent tools as well. You will come up with specific tactics that work for you. I often meditate on what I am feeling, then give the emotion a name. I then let myself feel it fully for a minute or two. Then I sit quietly, focusing on tense, painful muscles and my stomach moving with my breath. At first it felt awkward, but after a week or so of practicing this once a day, I stopped judging myself, and learned to let it led me to internal peace. Awareness of our emotions and mindful acceptance is deeply calming and amazingly healing. Now, take a few minutes now to record a few ideas, then try one out before you come back to this section.

◊◊◊

How does that feel? Empowering, isn't it? These skills *almost* become second nature after enough time and practice. Recognizing the need to manage a thought starts to come quicker as well. Be patient and keep practicing. Use methods that work for you and the situation you are in. Exercising your agency and the thinking centers of your brain takes power away from the distraction.

Now that you have ideas of how to stay in the moment, let's talk about why this is so important to do. I'll also clarify what I mean by "here and now" so you can really grasp what habits I'm encouraging you to develop. First, think back to a conversation where you did not feel like the other person was really listening to you. Maybe they were distracted by a passing car, their phone, or whatever. Do you remember how it felt? If you're like most women, it felt invalidating, like you didn't really matter, or weren't worth the time to pay attention to. When children grow up in an environment where they are not really heard and seen, it affects them. They don't value their own feelings or needs. Often, they stop even being aware of those needs. They take that unawareness into adulthood, and unintentionally create the same environment for their own children. Few people become aware of the cycle and find a way out.

Without changing habits intentionally, living in the here and now is impossible. We must find ways to connect to the moments, and anchor ourselves in the present with those we love. Just deciding is a huge step, but it is also the easiest step. You'll need a plan, habits to help you stay connected. It's funny, when I first started trying to stay in the moment, I almost thought I had ADHD. Focusing on one thing, and only one thing, for five to ten minutes was *hard*! We are used to hearing the television, answering text messages, and making dinner at the same time. Slowing things down can feel like the world has stopped turning. It hasn't. The pace of life does move quickly, but there is always time to really see another person. Taking time to do that also makes it easier to see ourselves more clearly. As you learn to tap in to what is going on around you, needs seem to bubble up. These can be your needs, or those of someone close to you, right in this moment. They can be the needs of a stranger as you see a new neighbor unloading a truck. Without taking time to feel what is inside the moments of life, these opportunities pass by all too quickly. You do have a choice, however. Again, it takes practice. If you want to learn to see the world more completely, and experience more happiness, clear the clutter in your mind and schedule. Then sit on a park bench and listen to children play. Let the thoughts of work and chores to be done just go. Be in the moment, and feel the peace come. It is so worth it, and you might find yourself recharged, too.

Take a moment to sit back where you are. Just listen to your breath, eyes closed, book down. Spend a few minutes just feeling what is going on in your body. How does it feel to be sitting where you are? Is your neck tight? How do your hands feel? You will be amazed at what being fully present in your body will do for your mental state. Try to practice this for a few minutes two or three times a day. See if it makes a difference in your stress levels.

One final thought. I want to offer a word of caution about relationships or events that encourage you to distract yourself. Some aspects of life are easier to deal with or more enjoyable. If certain conversations, people, or places are especially challenging, that is up to you to manage. Controlling parents, advice-giving siblings, or nosey friends can be especially triggering. It is not uncommon to need to spend less time (or no time) with these people or in these places, especially early in the process. A life of integrity doesn't just mean you manage yourself so well you don't ruminate or fantasize. This kind of life also means you don't put yourself in harm's way physically, sexually, emotionally, intellectually, or in any other aspect of your life. Being in environments, listening to music, or watching movies that trigger those thoughts cannot have place in your new life. What is your motive for keeping these relationships? Why do you keep putting yourself in these situations when they jeopardize your recovery? Some relationships and places may be safe later, but for now, if you want to live like you say you do, there can be no justification for bringing those emotions up in yourself knowingly. You don't have time for that kind of distraction. If you do intentionally or knowingly jeopardize your here and now connection, these lapses (failure to protect yourself) need to be reported to an accountability partner. If you actually indulge the thought or behavior in any way, the relapse (engaging a compulsive behavior) also needs to be reported, with accountability for putting yourself in a compromising situation. This might sound extreme (or terrifying!) but I promise you will be glad you got in the habit. You need to investigate why you keep going back to things that lead you to do things you say you don't want to do. This accountability will make honesty and staying in the present much easier. Below are suggestions for slowing down and connecting to the moment. I suggest trying a few out, making them part of your daily habits.

Ideas for learning to live in the moment:

1. Take time to think about how your closest relationships are going. Can you do anything in the next 24 hours to try to improve one?

2. Ask your intimate partner or closest family member or friend how their close relationships are going, and if there is a need they have that you may be able to help with.

3. Are you too busy? Are there things that can be removed from your schedule?

4. Are there things you can plan ahead, or do the night before, so that starting your day is less rushed?

5. Where can you carve out five to eight minutes to read a story or sing a song with a child in your life?

6. Consider setting a timer for two minutes a day to meditate and feel the sensations in your body. Build up to ten minutes twice a day. While it may seem like this practice will leave you with less time, you may be surprised at how much more you can actually do. Taking this time sends a message to your brain that time is on your side. Stress hormones decrease, and your brain can relax.

7. Sit with your eyes closed for a few minutes when stress starts to overwhelm you. Just closing your eyes slows brain waves down and spreads them out a little. Calming your brain calms everything else in your body.

8. Don't plan more in a day than you have the emotional energy for, or you will run a deficit. Just because

there is time in the schedule, does not mean you have it to give. Your mental state needs to be calm and available, or you will burn out and start getting edgy with others. Keep the cycle from moving forward by learning to not overbook yourself.

9. Find experiences with which to practice deliberate attention. Focus on the very act of simple tasks, like making a sandwich, then eating it. Count the strokes it takes to spread the peanut butter, then focus on the fragrance. Keep bringing your wandering mind back to the task at hand.

10. When distractions come up, acknowledge them, then tell your mind what to focus on. (i.e. "Yes, I do need to create a meal plan and grocery list. Right now, I am driving my son home from school, so I am going to focus on talking with him. I can grocery shop tonight after dinner.")

Not only will these practices help you slow down enough to connect to what comes up as you stop distracting and fantasizing, you will also find them helpful for years to come. Your family will love the increased and undivided attention. Yes, these are recovery skills, but they are also life and relationship skills. You can adjust them to fit your needs better or come up with your own ideas. Whatever you do, learn to take time to be where you are, and with the people you are with. It is challenging, even uncomfortable, in the beginning. Be patient with yourself. You will get the hang of it if you just let go and keep trying.

Chapter 8

Personal Responsibility

It is time for us to take full responsibility for our lives, past and present, without excuse. We must then take responsibility for our own future, knowing only we can decide what that future will look like. Others will impact us, but how deeply is up to us.

The concept of taking responsibility for yourself is probably not new. Most adults have a pretty good grasp of personal responsibility. The trouble with those of us who spend a good deal of time distracted, in our own heads, or thinking about other people, is the disconnect with reality. It can be easy to "forget" a commitment or appointment. We may also find it easy to excuse ourselves for no good reason.

One woman I worked with struggled to hold herself responsible for much of anything. As a thirty-year-old, she lived at home with her parents, worked odd jobs "when someone would hire her" and had no plans. She also had a dog, which she could not afford. It should not be a surprise that recovery didn't go very well. Our scheduled calls were often missed, or she was late. There were always multiple excuses for why she couldn't follow through with her commitments or goals. It was exhausting. No amount of love, late cancellation fees, or honesty from me about what it was like for me to try to help her did anything. She'd apologize, shame herself, tell me how she should just quit wasting my time. Well, I was getting paid for the time, but not by her, so I reassured her that was not the concern. The concern was her fiancé's money and her failure to follow through with that commitment to him. I finally had to tell her that I cared about her too much to keep watching her do this, and that she needed to be in a place to pay for her own appointments. When she was ready to pay for them herself, I'd love to start seeing her again. It was hard to let her go, knowing she may not get the accountability anywhere else, but that was her responsibility, not mine.

As women, we are raised to take care of others, be self-sacrificing, and not complain too much. (No one wants to be *that* woman!) Because we are natural caregivers, those roles are readily absorbed. The trouble is, we don't learn to have boundaries or that it is necessary to not take responsibility for another person. Only children have claim on others for their health and safety, but even then, they need to start learning personal responsibility early. If a child misbehaves, he needs the consequence, not his mom. If he doesn't turn in the assignment, he needs to miss out on weekend plans to deal with his bad grade. Yes, there is a needed level of support, and personal responsibility must be taught. Cultural expectations don't always back this up, as Mom is the one who receives that email home, "Please make sure Sammy gets his project done!" Mom and Dad are expected to take much of the responsibility for school work and learning, just because they have responsibility to raise the child. Raising a child well means teaching her to meet her own deadlines. As scary as it feels, natural consequences are best for this kind of teaching. By rescuing a child from these natural consequences, parents set kids up to live in a fantasy world where everything is comfortable. These children grow up to imagine the world as being one particular way and cannot cope when it isn't. I use this analogy for three reasons. First, adults don't usually need this same level of care-giving, and most of the people you interact with are probably adults. They don't need to be taken care of, and neither do you. You *can* and ought to take care of yourself, it is just more work and less fun than having someone else do it.

Second, it is an excellent way to demonstrate the distractions we set up for ourselves when life doesn't feel fair. If it hurts, or we don't like it, we start thinking about how things "should" be. Fantasy enters in, with its Siamese twin, comparison. We may think, "Well, her parents paid for college, bought her a car, and she has a great husband. I deserve the same awesome life. Why is she so special? This isn't fair, my life shouldn't be this hard." Why shouldn't life be this way? Who said? That statement has no basis in reality, because life *is* this way. Only fantasy says differently. Sure, it may feel unfair and we may be good people who work hard. As tempting as it can be to compare though, comparison and declarations of "life isn't fair!" do nothing for us. They don't move us forward in recovery, and certainly don't win friends. The final reason I use this example is to encourage you to look at how you see the world, then language it when things don't go how you feel they should. The way a woman talks about the world around her is a major indication of how she sees any challenge. Are your words self-motivating and empowering, or do they blame others, making excuses?

The condition of your life now may not be what you had planned, but a little at a time, it was created. We make decisions all along the way that lead to the here and now. If something doesn't change, the future will be much like the present, only more frustrating because not much has changed. Women are also creators. Our power to create as human women is rivaled by no other collective on Earth. Sometimes we fail to recognize this power, which allows our fantasy worlds to take over, leaving the real world in disarray and neglect. While this is creation by neglect, it is still creation, and it is still our responsibility. Of course others in the household, especially teens and adults in the home, have responsibility as well. That does not excuse our lack of connecting to the needs in the home, or our failure to follow through with commitments. If we don't keep commitments with those who depend on us most, chances are we don't keep them anyplace else, either.

Recognizing that you can take responsibility for you, and outside of parenting, you are not responsible for others, is so freeing! Take a minute to just sit with this thought: "I can only choose for myself, and I only *have* to choose for myself." You only choose for you.

With that power comes great responsibility as well. It also means every choice is yours to take responsibility for. Aside from illness and some injuries, or being a crime victim, just about everything else is a choice. Though even then, sometimes it might be your choice, like the time I didn't lock my car. Someone stole hundreds of dollars of tools from the trunk. I didn't choose to be robbed, but I also didn't lock the doors. See what I mean? Facing the parts I can take responsibility for gives me power. The rest was taken care of by the police. We haven't had things stolen from an unlocked car since. Why? Because I decided then, if someone was going to steal from me, it would not be because of a decision I made. Our other two break-ins were 100 percent not my decision. Still sucked, but it sucked less.

As you learn to live a life of integrity, look at places to take responsibility more than you do now. Make a list and start with one or two small items. Get good at those, then pick more. This is one of the best ways I know to take back power and stop being a victim in life. I'll give you an example from my own life. Early in recovery, I caught myself making excuses all the time. Many of these situations didn't need an explanation, and the excuse was unnecessary. I chose to stop making an excuse when an explanation was not necessary (most of the time!). Then I committed to always be 100 percent honest. Sometimes, it was embarrassing. Once, I was late to a class I was teaching. Ugh. So, I walked in, set my things down, and stood in front of two dozen other adults, one of which was a surprise evaluation. I was blushing from the shame but didn't care. This was my proving ground. "I apologize for being late. I was not feeling well and slept in longer than I should have. Thank you for waiting for me. If anyone is particularly upset about this, please don't hesitate to talk to me after class as I'd like to personally apologize. Please also know, I will be much more careful in the future. Any comments before we get started?" There was one. "Wow, Coach B., that was really honest. Thanks for that. Usually my professors just blow it off." Huh. I was willing to hear an upset comment, even have my evaluator correct me in front of my students. Nope. Respect all the way around. It's not always like that, but even when it isn't, living in integrity feels so much better than a lie or excuse, even when it means being railed on or failing an evaluation.

Your level of responsibility will create your future. Are things headed where you want them to be going? If not, what needs to change? Are you letting past hurts and upsets keep you stuck in the past, blaming others? Please stop doing this if so! Only you have the power to truly ruin or rock your life today or tomorrow. It's true, others can have an impact. But girl, you have to decide what you want and start moving toward it. You have to start doing things differently now so you can have a better next week, next month, and next year. It takes time to get used to thinking this way consistently. I even want to make excuses some days. It is so tempting! I don't want to live life by chance though, so I stop making excuses the moment I realize that's what I'm doing. Old habits can be hard to get out of, but this one is worth every effort.

The past is tricky to take responsibility for. Childhood brings all kinds of crappy stuff. I'm not suggesting taking responsibility for abuse or other events that you had no say in. I *am* telling you that you get to decide how to feel about them now, and how much you let it impact your life for good or bad. Bullying sucks. Losing parents does too. So many events can happen and impact happiness. The long-term effects these events have, however, really are more up to us than we often realize. Learning from them and moving forward is a choice. The decision is sometimes painful, but moving on does not mean it didn't matter, or will stop mattering. It just means not staying stuck, instead choosing to love yourself enough to let life continue.

The same is true for mistakes you have made. History is part of the package of life. No one reaches the place you have without regrets. In fact, I'm fairly certain no one reaches 25 without significant remorse over something! The end of this section has suggestions for journaling prompts that I encourage you to take a look at, even if you feel pretty clear on the past. Regrets, the past, even really crappy choices, do not define you, and they do not need to hold you back. Let go and learn to love the person you are becoming, while forgiving the person you have been.

Sometimes taking responsibility with another person is possible, and some apologies cannot be made. Whenever possible, do attempt to make face-to-face apologies. Acknowledging your part, not making any excuses, and offering the sincere words, "I'm sorry" is the best formula. Then allow the other person to share their feelings. As they do, the door to honesty for both of you opens wider, and both hearts can heal. Offer more validation, acknowledgment of your words and actions, then apologize for additional things that come up, if you are ready. If not, just acknowledge you need time to process it, and that you will talk with them again.

As you learn to see your past, good and bad, more clearly, and love yourself in spite of it, your recovery from distraction will also get easier. Unspoken apologies fester. Once you get those out, you'll be so glad you did. Just be sure you run them by a responsible support person to take out all semblance of an excuse. It is common to need to have your hurt feelings around events heard and validated before you can take responsibility for your part. That's okay. Nurture yourself, heal, find someone who can hear your pain, then offer your regrets and accountability to others. As it feels safe to do so, it is also acceptable to be honest about your feelings around the event and the other person's actions. Don't try to offer your apology at the same time you seek that acknowledgment. People who are personally responsible will usually offer their own apologies when you do. Don't go into the conversation expecting that. Just know what you would want to say if it is offered.

This may feel like a lot to take in at once. My suggestion now is to take a break and go through a few journal prompts. Pull a few of the questions below that resonate with you right now. Write about them, set a timer for five minutes each. Don't overdo it but do get some of those emotions out and on to paper. They will feel less overwhelming. If you don't feel overwhelmed, at least take a short break to get a drink of water and use the restroom. There's a whole lot more responsibility taking coming up, and I don't want to overwhelm you with it all at once!

1. What events in your past do you struggle to take responsibility for?

2. Are there any actions you worry might come back to haunt you from the recent or distant past? (Consider separate inventories on separate paper for distinct time frames.)

3. Who do you blame for how your life is, or events, and what do you blame them for?

4. Do you ever wonder, "What if…?" and about what? (Consider this for things that did and did not happen, like "What if my friend had not moved away, passed away, etc.")

5. Sit quietly, and let your heart speak to you. When your mind tries to wander, gently call it back into focus, in a meditative inquiry. What else is hiding behind the curtain of your compulsive behaviors and the obsessive fantasies?

Give yourself time. I found it helpful to keep a running list I could add to. This is true for any inventory I have done. You will know what you need to do. Realize, until you see what you are afraid to acknowledge, your recovery will never be as deep as it could be. There will be festering slivers of secrecy and disempowering omissions.

Now, take a break for a little self-care and connection with someone who loves you. Come back when you feel ready. If you're ready now, rock it, girl!

Feeling ready to learn more about the gift of personal responsibility? Just remember, you are not doing all of this at once! You will want to re-visit this chapter often for more ideas. It's not always easy, but I promise you, it is absolutely worth the weight you will feel lifted. This weight can be historical (coming from your history), and the act of taking responsibility in your day-to-day life is incredibly empowering.

It probably does not need to be said but is still worth mentioning again. Your lapses (crossing bottom-lines, like "I will not watch romantic comedies because I compare my real life to them, and it takes days to feel happy again") and your relapses (watching the movie, then letting yourself fantasize or compare your marriage) need to be reported. Taking responsibility to someone who will hold you accountable and still express love to you will encourage you to do better. Let me clarify a little. Taking responsibility is owning what you do. It sounds like, "I chose to look for a movie on [movie provider] last night, found three I wanted to watch, two of which were romantic comedies. I put them in my queue. Then,

I justified watching one of the comedies because it had been a really long day at work, and I just wanted to unwind. I see now that I set myself up by even turning on the TV. That was a lapse. I then watched most of the movie. I did turn it off when the couple started to get intimate, so I'm actually pleased with myself for that. However, I still couldn't clear my head from what I had watched and can see it is time to just get rid of my [movie provider]. I do not like that I let it get from a lapse to a relapse, and do not want to do that again. I already called and cancelled my movie membership."

If you have good accountability support, she will respond to you something along the lines of, "Good awareness. I hear you have already held yourself accountable and taken preventative steps to support you in showing up for yourself better. Why do you think you felt it was okay to queue those movies? Did you think about not telling me? Why or why not? Are you considering any other steps to protecting yourself in the future?" She will hear you, ask questions, and send you on your way in love. She will never make excuses or let you do so. If you don't have women like this in your life, please find some.

Let's talk about one more important area of personal responsibility before closing out this section. No matter how hard we try to protect others from our compulsive thoughts, impulsive behaviors, and distracted way of life, we can't. Just because they don't bring it up or talk to you about it, does not mean your family and friends don't feel that you are preoccupied or acting a little more irritable than usual. It is literally impossible to act out with emotional (or physical) affairs, or act in with comparison, fantasy, and other forms of distraction, and not impact those closest to you. They have been affected. As you gain ground in recovery, you will begin to see the impact your distractions have had on others. Children are the most accurate manifestation of our inner lives. If there is distance, contention, anger toward you, or refusal to engage in conversation, you can bet they have felt your emotional absence. It hurts to see, I know. Before you go to them and try to fix things, work on your ways of responding to their hurt feelings and anger. Make sure you have it in you to hear their pain without defending yourself or making excuses. Also make sure you are fully committed to the changes that need to be made. It's even better if they can see how you have been working your program and are already adjusting your thoughts, behaviors, and responses. Then, when you are ready, ask them if the two of you can talk. Very young children just need you to change your reactions, then to start showing up better in their lives. Teens and adult children need more. They do not (and should not) know everything you have ever thought or done. An acknowledgment of your disconnection and poor behaviors is enough, coupled with a sincere apology and invitation to talk to you as feelings come up for them. Ask them what they need most from you now, and how you can make things up to them. It may be difficult for them to watch you change. Some people, your children included, may be unwilling to see, hear, or acknowledge the changes you are making. You will need supportive friends, and hopefully their other parent, to help you manage your emotions around those responses. Them not forgiving is not a reflection of you, it is a manifestation of their pain. That reality will hurt. Be kind to yourself, and don't let it sabotage the good work you are doing. Right now, my son is not really speaking to me. It hurts so much. I can't blame him though. I was totally distracted through nearly all of his years at home. We have memories, we bonded, but I did not give him nearly enough time early on. Now, he cannot forgive me, and cannot let go. I have to live with a person I love so deeply believing I do not love him as deeply as he needs. The untruths he believes are not my responsibility, but much of his pain is. I mean the early pain, not what he is in now. What he is in now, his decision to remain angry and hurt, is not mine. I have to live with it, but I also need to not take responsibility for those parts that are not up to me. I was emotionally absent when he was little. That hurt him. I did not get my act together before he was old enough to start blaming me for every pain in his life. And I did not repair the damage when I had the time. My shame and fear of losing him kept me paralyzed. I let it win. There is no going back, and until he is willing, there will be no moving forward. So, I love him from a distance, and as much as he lets me in from ten feet away. I'm not allowed to know where he lives. I hope that will change, but I don't have a say. I have apologized for not being there for him, for yelling too much, and for that time I punched a hole in the door in front of him. I was angry at his father, lost control, and he witnessed something I can never take back, something he never should have had to witness.

Do you see how I am responsible, and I am not? Do you see how you have responsibility, but how others respond is not yours to decide? I did not physically abuse him. He believes I did. I can apologize for the pain I caused, and I will not take responsibility for things I did not do. I can validate his feelings and fear from believing those things, and I cannot change his interpretation of my mistakes. It may be the same in some of your relationships. We must take responsibility for how we impact others, and we do not have to take abuse or responsibility for their distortions of reality. As you might imagine, I wish he'd hear me, see the changes I have made, and forgive. All I can do is love him and pray that things will change. It hurts, and that will not change. Then I realize, as odd as it seems, that I'm glad he is setting boundaries and keeping himself safe, even if he feels he must do that with me. I'm grateful, because if he sees me as dangerous to him and his future children, even if it isn't real to me, I know he will keep them safe from other threats, too. That helps a little, because whether he wants to admit it or not, I taught him how to hold those boundaries by holding my own. So, it is both. It hurts deeply that he feels this is necessary, and I am proud of him for keeping himself safe in ways he feels are best for him.

Chapter
9

Sacrifice and Service

REAL recovery requires sacrifice on our part and must include blessing the lives of others. Until we give up what we must, we will not recover.

Sacrifice

A client I had worked with for almost two years once said to me, "I cannot give up my smartphone. My whole life is on here. Plus, everyone at church will know I have a problem. Only people with pornography problems have flip phones." That took me back; she did have a pornography problem. And what does church have to do with the kind of phone she uses? We really do keep our lives in our phones nowadays, and perhaps we spend too much time worrying about why someone has the phone they do, or what they may be thinking about the phone we have. At first, I didn't have a response for her. At our next appointment, I did. "Well, you can keep it, but I'm telling you right now, you are choosing to let your addiction win." She quit coaching two weeks later. Her sobriety isn't what can be termed a recovered life. She chooses the phone. That's okay with me, I still love her, but I will not coach her again until she gives up that phone, and she knows it.

Sacrifice of beloved objects that can best be termed "security blankets" is hard for all of us. I thought I would *die* when I went off social media. And giving up my male therapist for a woman led to weeks of unpleasant withdrawals that included vomiting and ridiculous mood swings that made my shakes worse. But I did both, and I lived. The withdrawals subsided, and the obsession calmed to a low roar. I now use social media for business and have strict boundaries for social interactions on it. My new therapist was an angel, and a wise choice. Oddly, and for the first time, I learned what it was like to be attracted to a woman. We worked through it because she knew I wasn't truly sexually attracted to her, and though therapeutic boundaries are in place, I now consider her a dear friend. But I do not wonder how my previous therapist "crush" is, nor do I wander social media with him in mind. We are both part of a common community group. I am cordial, even friendly, and the feelings I once obsessed over for him have subsided. He and I don't hang out, and we certainly no longer have vulnerable conversations. I can care, wish him well, and even see him at events. It is all done from a distance though. I have no desire to test the adapted AA adage, "Once a drug, always a drug." There is no reason to go there. Knowing where I have been and where I want to be is protective, so I choose to focus forward. It helps that I did tons of work on that relationship, am healing my marriage, and did not see him or have contact for over five years. Plus, he has great boundaries and has learned a few things about working with attachment-traumatized women ... especially the "love addicted." I would not even imagine being this involved with any of my other former targets. That being said, he and I are in no way involved outside of a common interest and occasional small talk in a group of common friends. Do I consider him a friend? I think appreciated colleague is more appropriate. After all, I go to lunch with my friends. A former target, a former therapist crush, or a male colleague are not people I would go to lunch with anyway. Be careful who you term "friend." Your heart needs that protection.

This is probably hard to hear for a few of you. Others may be saying, "I don't relate. My drug of choice is pornography, fantasy, or (fill in the blank)." And I'm telling you, you have sacrifices to make too. When we justify in recovery, we do not obtain recovered lives, and we certainly fail to live a life of integrity. Justification is an excuse. Many women in situations similar to yours make other concessions. Smart phone sacrifice, tablets, filtering and accountability software and other safe guards are necessary. More than once, I have held the password to a client's accountability software or smartphone browser. After the second time having one just get a new device, I realized these passwords need to be held by someone more present in everyday life, like a parent or spouse. Better yet, the devices should probably not exist in these clients' lives, so those are the conversations we have. No one is excited, but a woman who truly wants to stop compulsive behaviors from ruining her life is willing to do her part. She is okay with not liking it and learns to appreciate the sacrifice instead.

It's all about what you are willing to do, not what feels comfortable. A recovered life is one where we call the shots, not our devices, browsers, or social media interactions. For example, a woman who lusts and fantasizes at the gym can either get a membership to an all-woman gym or use a friend's treadmill. It comes down to knowing what makes staying sober hard, then building safeguards around those challenges. These safeguards prevent lapses, and if you never lapse, you stay away from relapsing.

What is your challenge? Where are you lapsing (making poor judgment calls that make it easy to relapse)? The further from a relapse you can keep your boundaries, the easier you make it to stay honest and sober. As you move further from relapses, have fewer lapses (remember, those are the little ones that make relapse possible), the easier your accountability gets. This is where I like to high five my clients a lot, because if I don't have to spell out for you what you need to boundary, girl, you are in recovery, not just sober. If we are willing to give up what needs to be given up, even with a little sadness, then we are sacrificing something enjoyable for something so much more beautiful and worthy of our time. When we can do it without being told what needs to be done, we are self-aware and rocking some serious recovery mojo!

Sadness and Loss

Let's talk about that sadness for a few minutes. Giving something up is hard. It can produce very real, deep feelings of loss. Don't underestimate those feelings, and don't pretend they are not real. In fact, I want to validate how real they are. You've grown to cherish, take amazing care of, even "love" this little electronic companion. It means a lot to you. When you feel lonely, bored, anxious, upset, or sad, you reach for it. We bond to our devices. We decorate them, buy them cute cases, attach stickers and emblems of our other favorite things, and some of us even name them. I've done it! I had an adorable green laptop. It was slim design, only weighed 3.5 pounds, and had my life on it. Her name was Clara. My friends, I literally cried after accidentally dumping a full glass of water all over her keyboard. She never recovered. I was devastated. Now I've had to get a new one. And I've had two since. Clara is still my favorite. Granted, the sacrifice was more of an accidental burnt offering, but my computer was dead nonetheless! And every time I had to enter a password or find a file on my new machine, I felt a little twinge. Clara knew me, she understood me, and I was not happy she was gone. And you know what else? She was not a she, it was just a cutely covered collection of wires, soldering, and plastic. Ultimately it was my security and the ease with which I could accomplish my homework or write for my blog that I missed.

Learning to live without that ease while learning a new device that wasn't nearly as cute bugged me. It wasn't comfortable. The keyboard was different, it didn't stand out on my desk like my last machine, and I couldn't take it with me nearly as many places. But I got used to it. Now, this machine is just as familiar as my green one. I can work with it, and things go great. Better, even, because this one is faster and has a lot more storage space. And it is heavier. There is always a tradeoff. And we eventually adjust. It will take time, but you will adjust.

I hope you know me well enough by now to know that I am drawing parallels and trying to teach you something. My friend, this has nothing to do with your device, phone or otherwise. This has everything to do with how you distract yourself from real life, and how you feed your inner fantasy world. If you have a relationship with anything or anyone that numbs, distracts, or distorts your life, this is my way of encouraging you to take a look at what needs to change. What do you need to spend less time doing? What is being neglected, and why? Where do you go when you get bored, stressed, or lonely? Answers to these questions will guide your sacrifices far more accurately than I ever could, even if we've worked together for years. Get curious, then be brave. Empower your life of integrity by sabotaging the power of what keeps you from it. When you must give up a relationship, it can be even more painful. This is normal. Mourn it, validate yourself, but do not stay in this space. No matter what you feel right now, he is *not* your soul mate. He is a distraction from something else.

Service

It was entirely possible to incorporate service differently, but it goes so nicely with sacrifice for so many reasons. Giving of ourselves to help others takes energy, time, and sometimes money. I don't know about you, but I don't have a ton of any of those, and when I do, there are always other things I'd rather spend them on. Except service, or giving back to others, is required for the recovery of your life and mental energy. If we do not learn to serve in recovery and life, we become self-absorbed and can easily stagnate. Have you ever smelt stagnant water? It stinks. No one wants to take a bath in that, let alone take it into their bodies. Our lives can become like that without service. If the service causes us to sacrifice and stretch, all the better. In stretching to help others, we gain more compassion. We also come to appreciate what we have and can do more. Not to mention, we could all use a little healthy distraction when trying to replace the obsessive fantasy or compulsive sexual behaviors of our vices.

In twelve-step programs service in the group community is built in through sponsorship. This allows members to build relationships, hopefully of trust, to serve, and to be served. I have facilitated and organized a number of twelve-step based groups over the years and have come to truly appreciate the necessity of service in recovery. When I first started sponsoring in my own recovery from compulsive relationship behaviors, I was blown away at how my own recovery work deepened. These weren't just random people I was talking to, they were sisters in recovery, and they mattered. The advice, encouragement, and hope I wanted to share needed to be right on, because they trusted me. I wanted to do right by them. It was a sacred space to stand in, and to this day humbles me. Helping another woman along the path to her own recovered life is invaluable. Learning to lead and guide in kind, gentle, but fully responsible ways, feeds both souls in the relationship. When you have your own recovery well underway, it will be greatly blessed by reaching back and lifting another woman on the path. It is incredibly rewarding.

As women, we are usually serving in daily ways as wives and mothers, or as sisters and daughters. There seems to be something innate that drives us to offer assistance or a listening ear. These moments offer beautiful reminders of how we are all connected and meant to need each other. And they can be triggering when we feel taken advantage of. This is where service to self, also known as self-care, comes into play. You've probably heard the phrases that allude to our inability to serve with an empty tank, or how we can't make deposits into someone else's emotional bank account when ours is in the red. We need to take care of ourselves and set good boundaries around how much of our time or energy others can have. This is challenging when we have a lot on our plates and others who count on us. And we still need to find a way to do it anyway. For example, setting "appointments" in our calendars that block out time for spiritual nourishment, mediation, and inspirational recovery work helps me. This time is non-negotiable unless a kid calls from school puking. The phone gets silenced, the doorbell ignored, and my bedroom or office door gets shut (locked if necessary). Of course, my kids are older, and I don't need to worry about little ones who need me. That being said, if you want to find a way, you will. A woman determined can move mountains to make things happen, so get creative. No excuses, no justification, find the time to feed your soul. When our boys were younger, my self-care time meant taking a little extra time hiding in the bathroom, or I'd get together with a friend and we'd read or chat on her couch while our kids played on the floor. Then we'd play a game together while also taking care of our kids. Sometimes, oddly enough, more kids meant less need for Mommy or Grandma. You can figure this out! Ask friends and family members how they do it. Who knows, maybe you can trade once or twice a week.

Serving outside our bubbles of home and family give us incredible growth opportunities and the chance to make new friends. For a long time, I shied away from helping in homeless shelters and the like. It was my own shame at having more. Now, I see people who need a little love, just like I do. They aren't usually thinking about how much I have and judging me, so why am I judging myself? Others in need are often grateful and humbled by our service. Our attitude in service can help them relax and feel less shame. Ultimately though, our shame belongs only to us, and no one can give it to us or take it away unless we decide, even subconsciously, to give or receive it. Your compassionate, giving heart, when coupled with love instead of pity for those in need, will open the door to a soul-to-soul connection you will start to crave. It is intoxicating, but in the best, most non-addictive way!

Boundaries

It is important to mention a little about boundaries here. You can find more back in the chapter on Empowerment; this will just be Boundaries 101. For starters, service should not jeopardize recovery efforts. Some of us may tend to serve far more than is helpful or healthy, feeling if a little is good, a lot must be better. Not necessarily, especially early in the journey to a recovered life. We need to build up to working service into our recovery work, just as we need to build recovery work into our lives. It gets easier if we are consistent and determined. But don't forget self-care. Except on rare occasions after we already have good recovery under our belts, we need to not let service interrupt eating, sleeping, quiet time, and exercise. Having limits just means you are human. Setting good boundaries for yourself makes you a smart human.

Chapter 10

Gratitude

Gratitude, either unfelt or unexpressed, will keep us small and unaware of the beauty around us. Feel it, speak it, show it.

I'm sure gratitude is not a new concept for most of us. In fact, you probably have your own ideas about it already. I'd like you to take a few minutes and jot down what this value means to you.

◊◊◊

As women, we often struggle to find peace in a world with so much turmoil. The day-to-day stressors are enough to distract us. Add in our natural tendency to set goals, dream of progress and potentialities, and it is little wonder we get anything done at all. We have a deep desire to do and be more, to create more for ourselves and those we love. We want to matter, to aid, to uplift, to leave a legacy. We often feel selfish doing things for ourselves, so neglect the very person we need most: the woman in the mirror. We worry about making a difference, raising our children well. We don't realize that we are powerful co-creators with God. We literally carry the future within our bodies and bring it forth with little to no effort. It is almost as if we have been programmed to see ourselves as powerless, weak, and invaluable, when the exact opposite is true. We give birth to nations! We are creators. What, I ask, are you creating within your mind? Is it drama, or REAL relationships? One will move you forward, closer to God and the life you truly want. The other will keep you from living your life, trapped in a matrix of never-ending distraction. What, my dear friend, are you creating?

Do you compare yourself to other women in clothing size, temperament, and family status? Do you measure your home and children against hers? Is your husband constantly up against any man you meet, real or fantasy? Are you certain other women have it all together, and you are the only one with cluttered closets, old food in the fridge, and children who lack basic manners? Or are you just glad none of that describes you, as you rule your home with perfection? Either way, you are creating, and none of this is reality.

I'll tell you right now, as someone others often think has it all together, and is living the perfect life, we all have messes in our lives. Stop comparing. This is not love. It is destructive. It is fantasy, and it will continue to eat away at any chance you have of real joy in your life. Everyone has a feature on their faces or body they would change. We all need a housekeeper/vacation/better husband. Time to move on and talk about getting out of the trash heaps and living the life truly before you. If you want to be happy, you are going to need to spend a lot of energy living in gratitude, looking for what is good around you.

Gratitude is a gift given to us, even when we are the ones expressing it. It just does something for the heart and soul to feel and share love with others through giving thanks. Gratitude is a large part of learning to live in the present moment with those we want to love most. As you go through this chapter, I encourage you to keep a running list of others you need and want to express gratitude to and for. Alongside their names, record a few words to remind you of what they have meant to you. By making the expression of gratitude a daily habit, your relationships will be strengthened. More important to this journey, you will begin to realize how blessed and fortunate you truly are, right here and right now.

I'd like to share a personal story, part of my history you have not heard yet. In late 2016, I was diagnosed with a rare genetic condition that will slowly take my ability to walk. Thankfully it won't paralyze me, but my ligaments will cease to work, making control of my skeletal muscles nearly impossible for long periods of time (by long periods of time, I mean more than a few minutes at once). This diagnosis was neither a surprise, nor a crushing blow. Don't get me wrong, it sucks. But I already had a good idea of what I was facing, and I chose to focus on the truth. I made a list of why I was thankful for the diagnosis, and even my illness. This is in spite of the fact that few doctors know much about the progression of this disease, and there is no cure. We don't even really know how to slow it down yet because it is such a recent discovery, and so few people have it. At home though, we focus on the good that is coming from this.

1. Our children will have constant opportunities to serve their mother, should they choose to accept them.

2. They will grow up grateful for health, and I will have the chance to be an intentional angel of gratitude and joy in adversity.

3. I know I am not crazy. "Rare genetic disorder" is why my doctors kept sending me to therapist for psychosomatic conditions. Now I know the truth. My illness kicks in at puberty and ramps up at menopause. That explains so much!

4. I have a rare opportunity to be a light of joy in adversity to everyone I meet.

5. Others will have the opportunity to serve me, and service brings us closer to those we assist. It also brings us closer to ourselves and God. If I accept their service with grace and loving expressions of gratitude, even strangers who open my door for me can be blessed by our connection of love for each other. Our humanity will connect us, because I need their help, often. I would not give this up for anything.

6. My friends, family, church members, and I have the chance to spend a little more time together. I love connecting deeply with others. What a great excuse

to deepen bonds with those who are also willing to carry this challenge with us!

7. The richness of life and ability to do for oneself is a gift. My circumstances have granted me a new set of eyes for every willful movement of my body. I have come to love my body with a sacred, reverent awe. It has done so well for so long. Now, I cherish and honor its contributions (carrying four babies into my arms, raising those babies into wonderful men, loving daily, and holding my sweet husband close).

8. I'm being essentially forced to exercise, as that is what will keep my legs going longer. Sweet! Health, vitality, and lots of time for my favorite podcasts and 80s playlists! My health may not look like health anyone else really wants, but hey, look how much I *can* do to stay out of a wheelchair for a few more years. Not everyone has that option. What a gift that I do!

I could keep going but want to move on to you. What challenges do you face in your life that feel like they are keeping you from living the life you want? Make a list now, leaving space to add to each challenge later.

After you have finished this chapter, and even while you read it, I want to encourage you to jot down how your challenges have blessed your life or can bless you and those around you. Add additional challenges and roadblocks you may encounter on your way to your dream life. (*Not* your fantasy life, but your responsible, love-based dreams for yourself and your family). What hidden gifts might make this challenge one of your greatest blessings, if you can just reframe it as such? Take your time and listen to the feelings of your heart. Leave your head out of this, it won't serve you well here. Think, love, remember with your heart and soul.

Learning to be grateful for others in your life, and the good they can bring, helps re-connect you to those you love. Through your efforts, the relationships you now struggle with have the potential to turn around. Of course, it also takes willingness on the part of the other individual. However, you create a safe place for them to test a new dynamic when you express genuine gratitude and care. We all know what it is like to have a frustrating husband, child, in-law, or neighbor. In fact, it is also true others might find us frustrating. When you focus on what you *can* feel gratitude for, your energy in the relationship changes. Have you ever felt someone was upset at you, had them tell you they were not, then found out later they were? We often know what others feel about us. Practice being grateful for what others contribute to your life in your mind, through prayer and meditation and through journaling. When you feel ready, start to express that gratitude in low-risk situations. After all, grocery store clerks and mail carriers spend all day serving. They would probably love a "thank you."

If you really want to kick these exercises with gratitude into high gear, I can tell you how. Watch the world around you with your heart drawn out to what God is doing for you, then thank Him for little things. This practice connects you to a Power greater than yourself and heals the self-centered pain we pile up by indulging distraction. Early in my own recovery from anorexia nervosa, I was reminded to keep track of the good things around me. Then, as I started working on my relationship and romance addictions, I was reminded again. This time, my dear friend told me to keep a "God's Handbook." While this is a funny little play on words, it is also a miraculous way to connect with the wonderful moments life offers every day. I took the challenge and filled a journal she bought me with how I saw God's hand in my life from my very earliest memory. To this day, that little pink leather book is my most cherished token of recovery. It has brought me back to reality more times than I can count. Express your gratitude to and for something greater than yourself, daily. Seriously consider keeping a daily tracker of the little miracles and joys that come. You will be amazed at how your focus and outlook on life changes.

Going a little further, gratitude for recovery is also important. Recovery from our distractions, especially without replacing them, requires a change of focus and outlook on life. Be grateful for the people who encourage, support, and challenge you. Also find little moments and experiences to express written, prayerful gratitude for. Finally, learn to be grateful in the ups and downs of living a new life, without distractions. Withdrawals verify the physical and chemical dependence you have had on your drug(s) of choice, be it fantasy, house cleaning, washing your hands, anger, pornography usage, or a relationship. They tell you that you are right to be concerned. Withdrawals are not enjoyable, yet they can give you a physical focus outside of your head while you detox from whatever it is you are drawn to. If you start to feel a pull for new things (sweet or salty foods, arguments, too much sleep, disordered eating patterns, or anything else) your mind is clearing out the drug and trying to replace it. Good! It means you are working hard at recovery and can give yourself a high five! I found gratitude for my withdrawal symptoms actually made them less miserable. It was like my body was telling my emotions how much it understood.

Take note of those cravings and keep your eyes open for what long term recovery buffs call "pinch-hitting" new drugs of choice. Flirting may not be as "bad" as watching pornography and masturbating, but it can be just as intoxicating for the withdrawing female brain. Sexting may not be considered a "real" affair to some, but in your world of integrity, there are no excuses. Pay attention to what your withdrawals, cravings, thought patterns, mood swings, and physical sensations can teach you. Then, be grateful your body is giving you grief, because it means you are weakening the beast! When you have lapses, even when you relapse fully, good news! You now know what doesn't work. Be accountable to self, God, another person, and then make a plan. Don't use this as an excuse. Protect yourself better, manage your environment better, and learn from it. Even a relapse isn't a failure if you learn from it, then lean into deeper, more honest recovery.

Write about what you can learn and how you can be grateful, even in the worst moments. You will be amazed, again, at how powerful gratitude can be when fighting distraction. You can't help but come to a place of more peace and hope. While you are at it, give yourself a fist bump, big hug, and letter of gratitude. After all, without your efforts, your recovery will not happen. Be grateful for whatever drives you; your grit, and your stubborn streak. That stubbornness will serve you well when temptation pops up unexpectedly. Revisit this chapter when you feel especially down or frustrated. Grab an idea that resonates then get to work! You won't regret it.

Finally, I encourage you to write down and feel, deeply within you, gratitude for the truths you know, and want to or do believe. Do you know you are created after the image of God? Write it down. Do you know there is one person on Earth that will always love you, no matter what? List their name and why this matters to you. Do you know that you got yourself into this mess? Good! Write down how those choices, turned around, can also help get you out of it. What positive moral, eternal, sacred, physical, truths do you *know*? Make a list and let yourself keep going. Try to reach seventy-five, then 200. You know a lot more about truth than you give yourself credit for. After you have hit your target number, highlight the truths that can encourage you on this journey. Ask others what truths they know, and if those statements resonate in your soul, write them down. Meditate upon "truth" until you can feel yourself open up to all that the universe would teach you. Pray to see truth all around you. Truth is, after all, much like gratitude: it feels elusive, until you get the hang of it. After that, you can feel and see it everywhere. A note about truth: it is something someone else can identify and verify easily, or it is a deep feeling of knowing that brings you closer to others. It doesn't change, and gives a sense of empowerment and hope when properly viewed. If your "truth" doesn't do this, it might feel real, but it is most likely temporary. That's okay, temporary means you have room to improve permanently.

Gratitude may be one of the most important tools you will gain in living a life of integrity. Don't let it slip by you. A woman who judges or compares herself or anyone else is not going to find the depth of healing you are clearly seeking. I know you want this, because you have made it through this entire book, and have not given up. Gratitude undermines the power of the most seductive, tantalizing distraction. Take my word for it, then go take back your life! You deserve to be happy. Gratitude paves the way.

Chapter 11

A Call to Action

My friend, it is time to make some long-term commitments. I have a few tools up on HerRecoveryRoadmap.com for you. They are listed with an asterisk below. Others are ideas I encourage you to consider. You can easily develop your own trackers and questionnaires that will help you stay focused and honest. I'd like to encourage you to visit the website or choose one or two ideas from here and begin to take action. Spend at least twenty minutes a day taking action. This includes recovery reading, journaling, personal inventories. Speak to your accountability partner with a focus on recovery, not just connection. Call her for connection when you have completed your recovery work. Reading recovery blogs, writing your own, and being online in general need to not be part of these twenty minutes per day. This will help you stay connected to what you are doing, preventing distraction from the emotions that will naturally arise. Keep your phone in another room, and focus. Meditate, use mindfulness techniques, study, pray, and journal. The most important thing to do is keep moving forward in recovery, and don't let yourself stagnate. You will learn to walk the fine balance between working hard on your recovery and not overdoing it.

- Checklist, "Am I ready for Recovery?"*
- Ways to take responsibility when a face-to-face apology is not possible, or best for all involved.
- Healthy Distractions/Here and Now, PDF*
- Investigative Questions, PDF*
- My Favorite Mindfulness Techniques
- Trigger Tracker
- Accountability Tracker
- Daily Inventory Tracker
- Responsibility Questionnaire*

The Cost

Before we close, I want to ask what solving your problems with distraction might cost you. What is it costing right now? What has it cost you already? What will the cost be next month, next year, in five years, in ten? What has been and will be the cost to you, your family, your children, your grandchildren, if you do not learn to manage this now? If you choose to keep indulging in fantasy and distracting patterns, everyone who loves you will be impacted. There is no way around it. So, what are you going to do about it? Are you, are they, worth your best efforts?

I know you can take this book and run with it. You probably have with at least a few concepts. Isn't it amazing to feel the power of change and choice? I think so, and have made self-improvement a permanent part of my life. I want to invite you to do the same. Yes, you can do this on your own. And I would love the opportunity to talk with you and determine if we might be a good fit to work the program together. It is invaluable to have someone to report to and learn from who has already been there. These principles have cost me tens of thousands of dollars, thousands of hours, over seventeen therapists and coaches. If you are considering working with me, visit my site to take my pre-call assessment. Then let's go from there.

Chapter
12

Closing Thoughts

This journey will not happen overnight, and it will not always be easy. You, however, have what it takes, and will succeed if you choose hard work and a whole lot of faith in yourself.

Obstacles

You will encounter obstacles, this is a guarantee. Triggers will show up from out of nowhere, things that were never an issue will seem to come at you from every side. You may be tempted to overdo it in recovery and tackle the whole beast in a week. Don't! Read the whole book through, getting to know the program and concepts overall. Then, take each chapter a week at a time. Take two weeks on the longer or heavier chapters. Do not take more than two weeks on one chapter. You will be tempted to stay where it is comfortable. Don't! Stretch. Move on.

You can always come back to a value and will hopefully go through this book many times. Do not get too comfortable, it will eventually jeopardize your recovery. Keep recovering forward, then circle back again to go deeper and get new ideas. This book was written to be used over and over again as you create your new life.

A Word about "User Dreams"

Every day brings new frustrations and awesome wins. The dreams might feel like they will drive you nuts. This is pretty normal. The majority of people who spend a great deal of time mentally focused on one thing know that it often shows up when they are asleep. There is nothing wrong with you. In fact, it is quite the opposite. If your brain is trying to steal a hit of fantasy in your sleep, you're probably starving it while awake. That, or you had an unresolved trigger you can now focus on to clean out and get rid of. Just don't get rid of it by picking up another compulsive habit! The last thing you need is another compulsion to distract you from the pain you've been hiding all these years. It will not feel like it, but you can absolutely conquer this. The values I have given you, coupled with your honesty and focused effort, will support you in replacing the distractions with a reality you can deal with. If you feel like quitting every fifteen minutes, that is excellent news! It means you are detoxing. Same thing holds true of user dreams and mood swings. Things will get better, a little at a time. Focus on how far you have come and the changes you have made. Don't let the road ahead minimize the path already trod! Stick it out, even in the uncomfortable moments of detox and withdrawal.

Speaking of detox, it calms down. Withdrawals ease up and the craving start to space out more. They also become less intense, lasting for shorter and shorter amounts of time. I remember coming down off a fantasy relationship I'd indulged mentally for years. I literally knelt, facing a corner, rocking, sobbing, and dry heaving. I wanted to just die. This was not a pretty cry. I'm talking snot and tears and whatever the crap else my body could throw out. This was brutal and felt like it would last forever. I was sobbing my apologies to God, my family, myself, the lonely little girl inside of me, and swear it lasted five hours. When I finally calmed down, washed my face, and laid down to recover, it had only been thirty minutes. Talk about a time warp! It is always more intense when you are in the middle of it. Episodes like this are few and far between. In all my years of distracted living, this level of ugly cry only happened twice, and both with a relationship I had fed for a very long time. The other three times were during major trauma healing, and a PTSD breakthrough. The last time I had to go through the loss (and girl, it absolutely felt like a loss), there was a lot of time spent with friends, family, and re-reading my favorite book series (no romance, and certainly no sex!) While a new distraction like a book series isn't always a good idea, this was one I knew was safe and would not hold triggers for me. I would only give myself until the pull into fantasy, to send an email, or to call, passed. Stopping mid chapter when my family needed me was easy. If you can't do this, no books. In fact, TV and movies, unless they're rare, with my hubby or kids, and boundaried (I will only watch one episode), are probably not a good idea at all. Better safe than sorry on the compulsive drive to watch "just one more."

It will take huge amounts of willpower, which you probably won't have at first. Walk, run, lift weights, listen to podcasts, or blare your Ace of Base! Okay, blare music that works for you – I'll use Ace of Base! Just make sure you are not triggering or indulging yourself. If certain songs, programs, or types of movies trigger you (ahem, romantic comedy is out!), they need to be given up. This might be permanent; assume that it is. If you are not willing to give these things up, you are going to relapse harder and more often. Not being willing to give up what must be given up is a gigantic obstacle to the life you are trying to create. Now is the time to commit and prioritize if you didn't in the chapters that covered sacrifice and responsibility. This step is hard for us all, and absolutely necessary. You will survive, though you might wonder at times. Hang in there.

Fear of Failure

Fear of failure is a common obstacle as well. We want to do right, clean up the messes we've made, and be perfect at it. My dear, you will screw up. You will fail. So what? Get up, dust off, and get back to work! Failure here is critical! How else will you learn how and when you need to do more to protect yourself? Failure is good news because it gives you more information. If this pisses you off, also good news! The intense emotion means you are serious and want to succeed. Good. Failure is not lack of success unless you give up. Quite the contrary, slipping up (lapsing or relapsing) is a gift. This is not permission to act in or out, but it is supposed to help you relax a little when you do. It happens. Learn from it and move forward.

When I don't do as well as I'd like, or I catch myself in a lapse, I refuse to beat myself up. Instead, I ask a few poignant inventory questions. Adjust them to fit your needs. I'll run through what this might sound like.

1. **What just happened and why?** I just caught myself thinking about the actor from the movie last night. It brought up romantic and sexual feelings that I want to indulge. This happened because I did not stop watching the movie when I felt these feelings arise. I did not protect myself when I caught myself feeling attracted to him.

2. **What do I wish had happened instead?** I want to get better at catching myself before I'm too tired or mentally drained to make good decisions. It would have been so much more helpful to have taken a hot bath and gone to bed early.

3. **What didn't go well?** I did not turn of the television or change the channel. I stayed up past ten, which I committed to myself I would not do, and I did not hold my no-romantic-comedy boundary. I used not knowing what the movie was about as an excuse.

4. **What did I do right?** I did shut it off without finishing the last thirty minutes, which I've never done before. I did not start watching something else. I got up, got ready for bed, and did recovery reading to clear my head. Then I went to bed.

5. **What would I do differently next time and why?** For starters, I'm going to shut off my cable. It's just too tempting. I'm also going to give away any movies I feel drawn to, or that have romance in them. I'd put them in storage, but that's just going to encourage me to pretend I can ever handle these kinds of movies again. I choose recovery, even though I hate that this is necessary.

6. **What am I going to do to make this up to myself and my significant others?** I'm going to stay away from electronic entertainment for three weeks. I'm also going to let my husband know that I lapsed last night, which almost led to a relapse today. Ugh! This sucks. I know he will be disappointed, but I would rather be honest than carry this alone. I've already talked to my accountability partner, she agrees I need to tell hubby.

Be honest. Say it how you feel it. Also, be responsible. A woman deep in recovery knows what boundaries she needs and has other women she can check in with for ideas. This is your journey, not your husband's or anyone else's. He should not have to come up with "consequences" for you. If he feels you need to do more, take it under advisement. If the boundary is so he feels you are really working on overcoming these distractions, seriously consider it. You made the mistake, you get to sleep on the couch.

Hope

Finally, it is mandatory you maintain hope. Fear of failure, withdrawals, loss of relationships, and keeping constant vigil on your thoughts is exhausting. If it feels like too much, give yourself credit for how far you have come. Focus on the progress made, without downplaying the successes. Do not focus on how far you have to go. Look just a little bit ahead to set goals, then take a small action in that direction. We all go through moments of despair; they are perfectly normal. In these moments, however, I want you to focus on gratitude. By doing so, you train your brain to jump from its reactive centers into its thinking centers. Push yourself. List as many things as you can in five minutes, make them into a song, or call someone and express thanks for a recent kindness. Heck, express gratitude that they didn't give up on you and walk away! Be honest. Yes, kicking the distractions out of our heads is hard work. They often border on (or are) obsessions. They won't go away easily. With your concerted effort, they will eventually become only memories. Find hope for the future by focusing on what you can be thankful for in the past and present. Then plan with goals (good, healthy fantasy!) Review recent wins you've had. Didn't eat two pieces of chocolate cake? High five! Totally a win. Also, make sure you are getting enough sleep and down-time to recover physically.

Eat well and try to stay away from high sugar foods. They are known to cause blood sugar plummets that make will power harder to use responsibly. Any of this can make hope hard to maintain. Don't give up. I know this journey hurts. I know it beats you up sometimes, and leaves you feeling totally abandoned. Call someone, send me an email. You can do this. Love yourself enough to go to bed and start fresh tomorrow, forgiving yourself for today. You are not alone.

My hopes for you

I hope, above all else, you choose a life of integrity and lasting recovery. The world needs more women willing to step it up and be beacons of light. I want to watch you, and other women like us, step in to the strength we carry. Women who choose to live these values, and embrace their power to create goodness, are unstoppable. Join us!

I also hope you will share this message. It's vulnerable. I get it. And there are other women out there, other women in your life, who need the hope and help that this message can offer. Share it courageously. I'm not asking you to put it all out there like I have, just offer the message when you feel it is right. After all, these values are not just for women who distract themselves compulsively. Anyone can benefit. Let go of fear and speak out.

I also hope you will embrace the risk of living a life of integrity. In integrity, we cannot justify living a double life anymore. When what is in your head comes into alignment with what is in your reality, the power and contentment is much more than you can imagine now. I'm telling you, it is so worth it! I truly pray that you, and every woman struggling in silence, find the courage to live how God created you to live: as His crowning creation, a woman who knows who she is, and who does not hide in shadows of distraction, justification and fear. You are worth more.

Review this book often, creating reminders in your life of how you want to live. My website has all kinds of resources, and I will be adding more. Read the blogs, listen to the podcasts, share what you love, print out and post reminders that will keep you on track. Most of all, stay committed to yourself by never giving up. Stay in contact with women who love you with responsible and compassionate feedback. You are worth recovery. You are worthy of love, forgiveness, and joy. Embrace your unchangeable value by always making time for self-improvement and growth. You will never regret it!

Live courageously, love without fear, stop the excuses, and value the woman you are.

In closing, I want to leave you with a few of my favorite thoughts. These little phrases, values, and principles have been hard won over years of recovery programs, more therapists than I want to admit, self-help books, and courses. I encourage you to take a few that resonate with you and put them up where you will see them. As you go along in your own process, create your own list.

– Yours in hope and recovery, Lacy

Lacy@HerRecoveryRoadmap.com

What I know for sure
- I am worth more than I can now imagine.
- I am worthy of love and joy.
- I am a Daughter of God.
- I have divinity within me.
- I am powerful beyond measure.
- My power to choose is my greatest asset.
- Just because I think it does not make it true.
- There are eternal truths, and my value is one of them.
- My compulsions do not define or represent the real me.
- What is, is.
- I give all people, events, and things the value they carry in my life.
- I get to decide.
- Don't play with fire.
- I define my future.
- The past cannot be changed.
- Here and now is the only place I can change.
- My choices today write my tomorrow.
- Tomorrow may never come, so I need to make today count.
- Children can never receive too many hugs or words of encouragement.
- Everybody could use a good therapist.
- Everybody is neurotic about something.
- Explanations are not excuses.
- There is no place in my life for excuses.

- Kindness is not permission.
- "Nice" does not always mean kind, or right.
- Boundaries and limits on how much of me or my time others can claim are mine to hold, and for others to respect.
- I can expect but may not coerce or force.
- Just because I think or feel it, does not make it the truth.
- An excuse is a relapse waiting to happen.
- This, too, will pass...if I do my part to change it!

Acknowledgments

I am grateful for the support of my amazing family. My husband Jon kept dinners on the table and clean clothes in the drawers, first while I got a four-year degree in three years, then while I wrote this book. I could not have done all this without him. Our boys were amazing, too. They learned to do their own laundry, clean bathrooms like pros, and *almost* clean the kitchen like Mom. Way to go boys, we did it! Hubsy, you are truly the wind beneath my wings. I'm am so grateful to get to grow old with you. The best is yet to be.

I've had amazing friends help along the way, too. Tonia brought food, Tennessa cleaned my house when I came close to losing my mind, and Brie kept me from giving up early on. Ladies, I owe you a Caribbean Cruise! Don't worry Bethany, you can come for being such a delightful editor!

To Mrs. F.N., you know who you are. Thank you for your insights, your wisdom, and for always showing up for yourself. We both know this book was really written for you, first. Much love and gratitude, my friend.

My launch and editing team cheered me on, listened to me whine, and gave a little tough love as needed. There are too many to mention here, but you all have the book now, you have my undying gratitude in print! I'm especially grateful for Jessica for the pep talks and encouragement only a friend of over twenty years can give. You freakin' rock, woman! Cheryl, you know who you are and what you did. I am so grateful we prayed each other into life and shared a backyard path as long as we did. Thank you for the serious butt-kicking when I needed it, and the hugs no matter what. And to my advanced readers, those who offered feedback, encouragement, and support from start to finish, Thank You! Especially my forwarding author, Forest, who spent many hours helping me prepare, then promote this little project. Reading his book gave me the push I needed to write my own, and he has been my biggest fan. Thanks, Forest!

I also want to thank Dr. Russ Gaede for his inspiration, council, and friendship. He taught me the principle of lapse vs. relapse used in this book. Thank you for being my first professional coach and such a great support. I look forward to our collaborations for women in recovery! Also, thanks to Dr. Paul Jenkins who first drilled home our innate power as human beings to create. "We are always creating, we never stop." -Dr. Paul

My mom, Nan, who has had a rough go, but inspires me by never giving up. My dad, Marty, who passed away before seeing the completion of this book. I know he is so proud of me, and high-fiving me to Heaven and back.

I'm thankful for my adoptive parents, Mike and Liz, who have loved me through it all, and kept every promise. I have no idea how I would have gotten through the last three years and made it here without you. God really does answer prayers.

Without the help of my coaching team at Author Incubator, I'd still be thinking about maybe starting this book. Thank you, Amari, Angela, Rae, and my personal cheerleaders, Cheyenne and Bethany. I'm also deeply grateful for the friendships I've made with other authors on this journey. What incredible game changers!

To the Morgan James Publishing team: Special thanks to David Hancock, CEO & Founder for believing in me and my message. To my Author Relations Manager, Bonnie Rauch, thanks for making the process seamless and easy. Many more thanks to everyone else, but especially Jim Howard, Bethany Marshall, and Nickcole Watkins.

And finally, to my Heavenly Father and Savior, Jesus Christ. Only You know it all, and how far I have had to travel to get here. How I love You and seek to honor You both in all that I do and say. May I, in some small way, be an instrument in Thy hands, for the good of others here below. You have made me so much more than I could have ever dreamed on my own while giving me a new Life. Thank You.

Thank You!

I want to thank you for picking up this book and loving yourself enough to make it to this point. Thank you for the work you do to bless others, protect your family, recover your heart, and live a life of integrity. To take the next step in recovery and get the support you deserve, shoot me an email at Lacy@HerRecoveryRoadmap.com. I'd love to hear from you!

Be well. Love well. Live well.

Lacy

P.S. Don't forget to visit www.HerRecoveryRoadmap.com often for new reader goodies and downloads. We have tattoos!

About the Author

L acy is Founder and CEO of Women United Recovery Coalition (WURC), an organization dedicated to raising awareness of female pornography addiction, how fantasy feeds sex-based compulsions, and women's unique recovery needs. She has been working with women in addiction and self-destructive compulsive behaviors since 2000. As an international best-selling author, a recovery mentor, coach, and speaker, Lacy focuses on releasing perfectionism in recovery while learning honesty, empowerment, and personal accountability. She has written articles and blogs for numerous magazines, women's recovery sites, and other leading organizations in the movement toward ending exploitation and fighting the harms of pornography on society. As a former Hentai (sexualized anime) user and relationship/love addict, Lacy has seen firsthand the destructive patterns fantasy can cause individuals and families. She also knows from personal experience that fantasy is the root of the sex/love addiction tree. Lacy avidly researches female sexuality and relationship and sex-based compulsive behaviors (what others call "addictions"). Her hope is to better inform about prevention, treatment, and recovery for the very real, very vulnerable population of women and girls trapped in their own pornography usage, fantasy worlds, and compulsive sexual or relationship behaviors. By attacking the roots of these behaviors, women and girls will be better armed to protect themselves, while developing healthy sexuality, free of shame or self-perpetuated abuse. Lacy's goal is to empower the next generation of wives and mothers to know and stand up for themselves sexually, without compulsive or self-destructive patterns. She currently has a bachelor's in psychology and is working toward a master's degree as soon as this book is all wrapped up! In her spare time, you will find her curled up with yet another book or research article and her "boyfriend," an almost five-foot ball python named Titus-Nagini. Lacy lives in the shadows of Utah mountains with her husband Jon, their four amazing children, a hamster, a leopard gecko, and way more feeder crickets than she cares to acknowledge.

Websites:

www.HerRecoveryRoadmap.com

www.WURCTogether.org

Email: Lacy@HerRecoveryRoadmap.com

Facebook: Lacy Alajna Bentley

@LacyAlajnaBentley @WURCTogether